LEKUAK
THE BASQUE PLACES OF BOISE, IDAHO

LEKUAK

THE BASQUE PLACES OF BOISE, IDAHO

MEGGAN LAXALT MACKEY

Center for Basque Studies Press
University of Nevada, Reno

This book was published with the generous financial support of the Basque Government

Basque Diaspora and Migration Studies Series, no. 14
Series editor, Xabier Irujo

Center for Basque Studies, University of Nevada, Reno

Copyright © 2018 Meggan Laxalt Mackey
Edition copyright © 2018 Center for Basque Studies

Cover Illustration:
The Basque Block, Boise, Idaho. Original photo courtesy Allan Ansell Photography.
Digital photo illustration by Meggan Laxalt Mackey.

Book design by Meggan Laxalt Mackey

Library of Congress Control Number: 2018959625

For Erin.

May you always know the power of place,

and the honor of "Being Basque."

For my immigrant grandparents Dominique and Thérèse Alpetche Laxalt,

and other first-generation Basques who braved journeys

from the Basque Country to the United States.

Their courage and persistence ensured a better life

for their children, grandchildren, and generations to come.

Dominique Laxalt baserri in Atharratze-Sorholüze (Tardets); Thérèse Alpetche Laxalt baserri in Baïgorri (Saint-Étienne-de-Baïgorry); Dominique Laxalt's "home in the hills" near Marlette Lake above Lake Tahoe, Nevada. Photos courtesy the Laxalt Family and the University of Nevada, Reno, Center for Basque Studies.

Cyrus Jacobs-Uberuaga boardinghouse, Boise, Idaho. Photo by Peter Oberlindacher. Photo courtesy Basque Museum and Cultural Center, Boise, Idaho.

CONTENTS

ACKNOWLEDGMENTS ‖ ix

PREFACE ‖ 1
Basques in the Old World
Basques in the New World

INTRODUCTION ‖ 9

CHAPTER 1 – BAT ‖ 15
Amerikanuak: Places by Basques, for Basques (Late 1800s -1920s)
Boardinghouses
Frontons
Church of the Good Shepherd
Conclusion

CHAPTER 2 – BI ‖ 37
Tartekoak: Bridges between Two Worlds (1930s -1950s)
Residences
Workplaces
Morris Hill Cemetery: St. John's Section
Temporary Places: Picnics and Mutual Aid Society Events
Boise's Basque Center
Conclusion

CHAPTER 3 – HIRU ‖ 71
Egungoak: Public Places of Shared Learning (1960s -Present)
Cultural Plurality on Display
The Influence of Education
Basque Museum and Cultural Center
Anduiza Fronton: Reclaimed
Basque Center Façade
Unmarked Basque Graves Projects
Boiseko Ikastola
The Basque Mural
Conclusion

CONTENTS

CHAPTER 4 – LAU || 85
Aurrera - Moving Forward (The Future)
The Basque Block: Public Cultural Expression
Preserving Culture: Basque Places in the Twenty-First Century

POSTSCRIPT: WHY BOISE? || 99

TIMELINE || 111

LIST OF TERMS || 119

BOISE: UNIQUELY BASQUE || 125
Boise's Basque Cultural Components

MAPS || 129
Euskal Herria (The Basque Country)
Ostatuak: Basque Boardinghouses of Boise, Idaho
St. John's Section at Morris Hill Cemetery Plots (1935 - 1950)

ENDNOTES || 135

BIBLIOGRAPHY || 147

TIMELINE PHOTO CREDITS || 155

ACKNOWLEDGMENTS

SEVERAL YEARS AGO, DR. JOHN BIETER CHALLENGED ME TO A JOURNEY. He encouraged me to pursue my passion for education by entering Boise State University's graduate program to earn my Master's Degree in Applied Historical Research, focusing on Basques. That connected me once again to another passion: books. I could not have graduated at such a late stage in life, nor accomplished *Lekuak* without John's guidance and patience. He convinced me that *Lekuak* would contribute to the greater body of scholarly work about Basques. He served as my graduate committee chair with his characteristic insight and kindness, always ready at a moment's notice to help me. John's wife Alex also unselfishly lent John to my personal and professional cause. They have remained dear friends through the years.

Two other professors formed my committee: Dr. Jill Gill and Dr. John Ysursa. Jill provided unique perspectives and steady encouragement to think outside the "Basque box." Dr. John Ysursa's expertise in Basque history and culture were invaluable. His natural intellectual curiosity led me to be a more discerning scholar, his persistence lifted me when I was exhausted, and his humor taught me how to lighten up.

Dr. Dave Lachiondo from Boise State's Basque Studies, and Dr. Xabier Irujo, from University of Nevada's Center for Basque Studies, both encouraged my thirst for learning more about Basque history and politics in Euskal Herria and the diaspora. Argia Beristain Dougherty and Nerea Lete taught me lot about strong Basque women, past and present.

Several other Boise State University faculty members were foundational to instilling my passion for history years ago, when I was an undergraduate with a small child and little means to finish my schooling: Dr. Todd Shallat, Dr. William Tydeman, and Dr. Erroll Jones (who is no longer with us).

Basques are a community of givers. Many in this circle provided time, expertise, and support. I owe a debt of personal and professional gratitude to my friends at the Basque Museum and Cultural Center. Patty Miller was with me when I decided to leave my federal public affairs career after almost thirty years to pursue Basque studies, and she's been through rough waters and smooth sailing with me ever since. Annie Gavica, Amanda Bielmann, Missy Thomas, Linda Morton-Keithley, Wendy Bauer (who is no longer with us), and Board Members Toni Berria, Connie Urresti, and Liz Hardesty helped me with this project. Later, Celeste Landa, a fellow Nevadan, teamed up with me on the Basque Graves Projects, included in *Lekuak*. Oihana Andion Martinez has been another steadfast friend and translator of many Basque

LEKUAK: THE BASQUE PLACES OF BOISE, IDAHO

words I am still trying to speak. Each of these Basques are deeply committed to preserving our culture, which makes me even more proud to be a public historian focusing on the Basques. Sharing history in this capacity honors our collective Basque heritage, and the heritage of immigrants from many ethnic groups who left their homelands and families for better lives in other places.

My dear friends Kay Schiepan, Pat Entwistle, Lynn Thomason, Kim Buxton, Jeff Johns, Bob Blesse, Jason Pyron, Deniz Aygen, Larry Ridenhour, Brian Kelly, Jack Sept, Jeff Foss, Wade Brown, and Mimi Richards Melarkey have always offered constant encouragement for this and other projects. Without Dan Montero, publications editor at the Center for Basque Studies, this book wouldn't have been possible, and thanks for the great editorial assistance of Carly Sauvageau.

Thanks to photographers Peter Oberlindacher and Allan Ansell for allowing me to use their beautiful photos, to the Basque Museum and Cultural Center for permission to reproduce so many historic photos from their collection, and to my daughter Erin Ann Jensen who also contributed her photos and creativity to this project.

My family has shown me love and support through all of my life journeys, including this endeavor. *Lekuak* was driven by the memory of those who have left this earthly world, but who will remain in my heart forever: my mother Kathi, my father Peter (Micky), my two brothers, Paul and Stephen, and deceased uncles and cousins. My youngest and only remaining brother, Rick, is now on his own journey, where he now lives not too far from our family's ancestral villages in the Basque Country. He is my source of courage to bravely try new things. My sister-in-law Theresa Mackey, cousins too numerous to name here, and grandmother Dorthella Silva have always been there for me through many, many years.

Lastly, but by no means the least, two amazing individuals have stood behind me with so much love and rock-solid steadiness: my daughter Erin Ann Jensen and my husband Dennis Mackey.

Thank you all for being a part of *Lekuak*. This has been a personal and professional journey about place — in honor of those who had the courage to take that first journey to a place far from home.

Eskerrik asko.

Basque Country baserri. Photo courtesy University of Nevada, Reno, Center for Basque Studies.

PREFACE

Basque village. Original photo courtesy University of Nevada, Reno, Center for Basque Studies. Digital photo illustration by Meggan Laxalt Mackey.

LEKUAK: THE BASQUE PLACES OF BOISE, IDAHO

Dominique Laxalt's family house in the Basque village of Atharratze-Sorholüze, in Zuberoa, France. Photo courtesy Laxalt Family.

BASQUES IN THE OLD WORLD

Nire Aitaren Etxea
Ni hilen naiz,
nire arima galduko da,
nire askazia galduko da,
baina nire aitaren etxeak
iraunen du Zutik.

The Family Home
I'll die,
I'll lose my soul,
my kin will stray,
But my father's house

will stand.

Gabriel Aresti, *Harri eta Herri*
(*Rock & Core*, translated by Amaia Gabantxo)

LEKUAK: THE BASQUE PLACES OF BOISE, IDAHO

A village in the rural countryside of the Basque Country. Photo courtesy Basque Museum and Cultural Center, Boise, Idaho.

PREFACE

GABRIEL ARESTI'S POEM, "NIRE AITAREN ETXEA," ("THE FAMILY HOME"),[1] uses the ancient Basque house, or *etxea*, that has stood for centuries to symbolize Basque cultural persistence. The etxea, village, province, and country bound Old World Basques together. These Basque places can be viewed as symbols of cultural endurance.

The Basque homeland, *Euskal Herria*, is a small region between France and Spain, near the Pyrenees Mountains and the Bay of Biscay. Some call the Basques *hasierrak* or "the mystery people of Europe" because although their presence in this land has been speculated since prehistoric times, the exact origin of the Basques is still unknown.[2] Some say the Basques may have originated during the Cro-Magnon period. Basques call themselves *Euskaldunak*, literally "speakers of Euskara." Euskara has unknown origins, and it is not related to any other Indo-European language, other than possibly Aquitanian.[3] Basques continue to define themselves by Euskara today.[4]

The Basques fiercely defended their place, which was reflected in their history of political, social, and religious conflict. They survived attempts by the Romans, Visigoths, and Franks to control their territory, which laid the foundation for the defense of Basque land and independence throughout history.[5] This was testament to their sheer determination to persist.

The Basque Country historically was comprised of seven provinces, termed "*Zazpiak Bat*" or the "seven are one."[6] Ninety percent of all Basques live in the four Spanish provinces of Bizkaia, Gipuzkoa, Araba, and Nafarroa. The remainder lives in the three northern French provinces of Lapurdi, Nafarroa Beherea, and Zuberoa.[7] It is a small place, only about 125 miles from end to end, although quite mountainous.

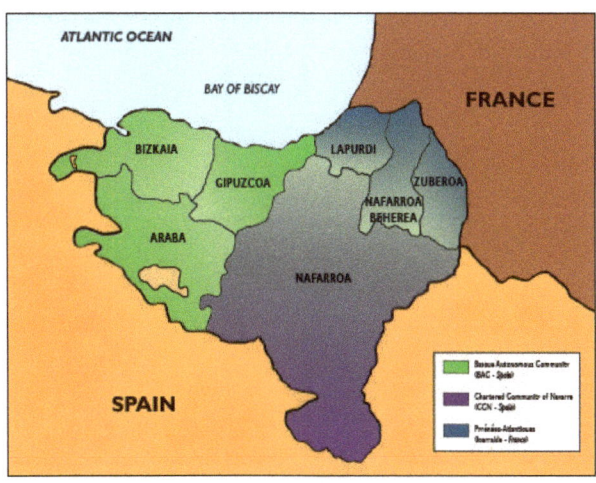

The seven provinces of Euskal Herria (the Basque Country).

Basques also have a long tradition of mobility. Although Basques loved their country, there were many forces that pushed and pulled them away. As mariners, merchants, missionaries, miners, and those involved in military efforts, they ventured far beyond their borders for centuries.[8] Basque whalers, ship-builders, and tradesmen were some of the first to navigate the oceans, beginning as early as the eleventh century and in earnest by the sixteenth century.[9]

Conflicts in places of migration and the homeland continued to shape Basque history. In the nineteenth and twentieth centuries, the bloody and brutal Carlist Wars (1833–1840, 1846–1849, and 1872–1876) and the Spanish Civil War (1936–1939) instilled deep divisions between the Basques and the Spanish, and fractured political parties and families for generations.[10] The oppressive Franco dictatorship further cemented political, religious, and social discontent in the Basque Country from 1939 until his death in 1975.

This long-standing history of Basque resistance to control their land and fight for self-determination caused great division in the Basque Country. It also forced the exodus of many Basques from the Old World to the New. Despite attempts to suppress them and control their land, Basques persisted in both their homeland and various diaspora locations. Mark Kurlansky claimed in *The Basque History of the World* that the "singular most remarkable fact about the Basques is that they still exist."[11]

Basque immigrants in early Boise. Photo courtesy Basque Museum and Cultural Center, Boise, Idaho, Arregui photo collection.

BASQUES IN THE NEW WORLD

Basques have a tradition of loving their homeland — and leaving it.

John Bieter, *An Enduring Legacy: The Story of Basques in Idaho*

Vintage postcard of Ellis Island. US GenWeb archives.

BUILDING ON A LONG HISTORY OF EXPLORATION AND SETTLEMENT, Basques migrated in the mid-nineteenth and twentieth centuries primarily to the western United States.[12] These Basques risked a move from their homeland to build better lives for themselves and their families, similar to millions of other European immigrants who also searched for improved fortune beyond their birthplace countries. The Gold Rush of 1849 drew Basque immigrants from the pampas of Argentina to California. Rather than gaining wealth from gold and silver, livestock opportunities prompted many Basques to venture into western states, particularly Nevada and Idaho.[13]

Later, brave Basques left from ports in Spain and France to travel an arduous journey for weeks by steamship across the Atlantic Ocean. These immigrants arrived in New York City and endured a sometimes humiliating processing at Ellis Island. In 1869, the new transcontinental railroad enabled faster, safer, and less expensive travel to the West.[14] This second and more-traveled route triggered a larger stream of immigration into the western United States. Most entered through Ellis Island, and some Basques settled in New York. Many chose to board trains for a five-to-seven day journey across the country to the American West, often with nothing more than sheer determination.[15] Work in the sheep industry in southwestern Idaho drew Basques to Boise. Most hailed from small villages of the Spanish Basque province of Bizkaia.[16]

LEKUAK: THE BASQUE PLACES OF BOISE, IDAHO

Generally, Basque males came first: usually poor, young, with limited education, and unable to speak English. Most intended to return to their homeland after "making it big in America," or at least with enough savings to eventually return the Basque Country.[17] Boardinghouses most often provided the first places in America for Basque immigrants. In this "home away from home," they could speak Euskara, eat Basque food, and learn about prospective jobs.[18]

Many men took jobs that most Americans did not want, for little pay, and in harsh physical conditions. The fast-growing American sheep industry drew Basque men to jobs as sheepherders. For most, this was a daunting experience, as they had only tended to a handful of sheep in rural Basque Country farms, or had no experience at all with animals if they had previously lived in fishing villages or the city. As the wave of immigration into the American West progressed into the 1920s, many Basques became part of chain migration that led to the first immigrants bringing their fathers, uncles, and brothers to join them as sheepherders.[19]

Some women were also summoned to America to join their family or friends, others traveled as brides-to-be. Although many boardinghouses primarily housed males, they provided economic opportunity for Basque women who worked as domestic help.[20] Boardinghouse proprietors filled the role of helping boarders navigate challenges such as language barriers, finances, and medical issues.[21] Boardinghouses linked two places: the Old World homeland and the New World host country. Eventually, the immigrant generation merged their Old and New World ways in their places of settlement in the United States, including Boise.

Boise today has a large concentrated population of Basques that have remained in the city for over a hundred years.[22] It has been a stronghold of Basque culture in the American West for over a hundred years, revealing this ethnic group's age-old ability to persist through time and place. In *Lekuak*, this story comes alive with the Basque Block.

The newest generation of Basques on Boise's Basque Block. Photo courtesy Allan Ansell Photography.

INTRODUCTION

The Basque Market's famous paella. Original photo courtesy Allan Ansell Photography. Digital photo illustration by Meggan Laxalt Mackey.

LEKUAK: THE BASQUE PLACES OF BOISE, IDAHO

The Basque Block welcomes visitors with two entry portals. These structures are steeped in Basque symbolism, each containing an oak leaf, a laiai (ancient farm implement for tilling soil), and topped with a total of seven red-green-white banners to represent the seven Basque provinces. Photo courtesy Meggan Laxalt Mackey.

INTRODUCTION

A street that connects who we were to the ethnic mosaic we are.

Todd Shallat and John Bieter
Becoming Basque: Ethnic Heritage on Grove Street

BOISE'S GROVE STREET TODAY IS A TREE-LINED STREET WITH OLD BRICK BUILDINGS, bustling with people from morning until night. Tandem structures that look like giant forks, at least fifteen feet tall, guard the street from Capitol Boulevard. These are *laiak*, replicas of ancient Basque farming tools for tilling the soil. Green, red, and white metal flags symbolize the seven Basque provinces. Two large green and red *lauburus* (ancient Basque symbols) are on the asphalt street, further symbolically connecting Grove Street with the homeland.

In good weather, restaurant patrons dine outdoors on Bar Gernika's patio, a postage-stamp sized Basque pub and eatery at Capitol and Grove. Visitors are often shocked to find a tall and deep handball court, a Basque *fronton*, that is hidden from street view next door at the brick Anduiza building. The Basque Market is cooking paella on the street in huge pans, scenting the air with garlic. Basque flags (*ikurriñak*) wave in the breeze, along with red-white-and-blue U.S. flags, in a colorful display of national symbolism. Granite blocks, each uniquely incised with Basque imagery, are inset into the concrete sidewalks. Seven different coats of arms represent each Basque province; four insets have Basque songs incised in them; and hundreds of Basque surnames appear on the sidewalk, coiled into a spiral shape around a single lauburu.

The Basque Museum and Cultural Center is adjacent to the Anduiza Fronton. It's easy to peer into the Museum's gift shop windows from the street. The Cyrus Jacobs-Uberuaga boardinghouse is a small brick home, sandwiched between

Basque surnames on the Basque Block sidewalks. Photo courtesy Meggan Laxalt Mackey.

LEKUAK: THE BASQUE PLACES OF BOISE, IDAHO

larger buildings on Grove Street. The tiny house is set back from the street with a white picket fence around a lawn and an oak tree. A bronze National Historic Register marker near the front door notes the home was built in 1864 by Boise pioneer Cyrus Jacobs, which eventually became a Basque boardinghouse in 1910.

The stuccoed, red-tiled Basque Center anchors the Sixth and Grove Street corner. Tambourine and accordion can sometimes be heard from inside the building, and dancers and musicians drift in and out for practices. *Euskara*, the Basque language, is frequently spoken here. Bar patrons enjoy drinks at the cozy Bar Gernika. Across the street, shoppers head into the small Basque Market that is loaded with specialty food and wine, and in good weather, a giant pan of paella simmers outside on the sidewalk. Next door to the Market, the Basque restaurant Leku Ona ("Good Place") invites Basque diners, and offers patrons a place to stay at their boutique hotel. Visitors can learn about multiple generations of Basques who have built their lives in this area by viewing interpretive signs on the buildings, too.

This is not a typical city block. It is Boise's Basque Block. It's the only cultural district in the United States dedicated to Basque culture. It represents a powerful intersection between people and place.

Lekuak means "places" in the Basque language. This book, *Lekuak,* traces how Basque places in Boise reflect the transformation of ethnic identity through successive generations. Today, the Basque places of Boise still remarkably represent Old World values that the first generation of immigrants from the Basque Country brought with them. These unique Basque places reveal at least one common thread: the Basque

The Basque Center and Bar Gernika. Photos by Meggan Laxalt Mackey.

INTRODUCTION

community or neighborhood, the *auzoa*.[1] In the Old World, maintenance of an auzoa was highly dependent upon communal work, or *auzolan*. This principle helped Basque immigrants resettle their lives in new places, or "new soil."[2] The concept of auzolan was foundational to the establishment and maintenance of new places outside Euskal Herria. *Lekuak* demonstrates how auzolan was applied to each successive generation's places, especially in Boise. Many of these Basque places remain today in Boise, in close proximity to one another so that they are more easily visible. There is no question that today's Basque Block represents the culmination of the evolution of Basque places over generations. Clearly, the Old World principle of auzolan, among Basques and non-Basques alike, helps to maintain this ethnic group's identity, and helps to preserve their places.[3]

Authentic Basque food and drink are highlights for visitors to the Basque Block. Photos courtesy Meggan Laxalt Mackey.

The evolution of Basque places can be understood more easily if each successive generation's places, such as places of work, are studied chronologically and divided into loose generational evolutionary periods. *Lekuak* therefore adopts this approach.

John and Mark Bieter applied a generational theory to their study of Idaho Basques through what they termed the *immigrant, hyphenated,* and *ethnic generations*.[4] The Bieters demonstrated that each generation exhibited specific traits, from a purely Basque immigrant group to a dual Basque-American generation, to a generation that engaged in the revival of Basque culture. *Lekuak* mirrors that generational look, and then applies it to *place*.

LEKUAK: THE BASQUE PLACES OF BOISE, IDAHO

The institutional framework established by Carmelo Urza is also helpful to understand the cultural transformation of Basque places in Boise. Urza's chronology contained the historical (1848–1948) period when Basques were generally isolated as a cultural group; the modern (1948–1967) period when the Basque social image was positive; and the postmodern age of institutions (1969–present) that saw the rise of Basque educational institutions, organizations, and clubs. [5]

Finally the societal phases described by William Douglass in *Global Vasconia* are helpful to better understanding this evolution (with some noted exceptions): first-generation immigrants who relied solely on their internal networks to survive; second generation Basques who reject their parental Basque ethnicity; and the third generation culture "seekers." [6]

The overarching eras of *Lekuak* help align each generation with historical events, and while not all generations, individuals, and time periods fit exactly within this schema, the following generational format is useful in order to trace the relationship between Basque people and places in Boise:

- **Chapter 1: The first-generation Amerikanuak** (late 1800s to 1920s) predominantly expressed their ethnicity as an internally focused, solely Basque ethnic group and built places such as boardinghouses and frontons that met communal needs.
- **Chapter 2: The Tartekoak** ("in-between" second generation, 1930s to the 1950s) mostly expressed a dual Basque and American ethnic identity. Tartekoak places often revealed the individuation of this generation with single-family residences and Americanized businesses, and the Basque Center with ancestry-based membership.
- **Chapter 3: The Egungoak** ("today" from the 1960s to the present) who may have mixed ancestral heritage, often express their ethnicity through conscious choice and inclusivity and principally created educational institutions that are also open to non-Basques, including the Basque Museum and Cultural Center and the Boiseko Ikastola preschool.

Boise's Basque Block represents the culmination of the evolution of Basque places over several generations. The visible, external expression of symbolic ethnicity today on the Basque Block validates the assertion of America's ethnic mosaic, the cultural plurality that includes Basques as a distinct and valued ethnic group. The persistence of the Basques within the larger society in Boise today challenges "melting pot" theorists who say ethnicity is on the decline in America. *Lekuak* documents Basque cultural persistence for over a hundred years in Boise, Idaho, through the lens of place. It begins with the Amerikanuak generation, internally-focused immigrants who initially settled in the American West.

CHAPTER I – BAT
AMERIKANUAK

Basque sheepcamp. Original photo courtesy University of Nevada, Reno, Center for Basque Studies. Digital photo illustration by Meggan Laxalt Mackey.

LEKUAK: THE BASQUE PLACES OF BOISE, IDAHO

Uberuaga family on the porch at 607 Grove Street, c. 1921. Photo courtesy Basque Museum and Cultural Center, Boise, Idaho.

CHAPTER I – BAT ‖ AMERIKANUAK
Places by Basques, for Basques (Late 1800s – 1920s)

Boise's Grove Street was a Basque enclave in this period. Indeed, there were so many recently arrived immigrants in the area that it was possible to start school speaking only Basque, since all of the children in the neighborhood were foreign- or American-born Basque-speaking children. Basque was the language of the home and of the streets.

J. Patrick Bieter, *Letemendi's Boarding House*

THE BASQUE TRANSLATION OF *AMERIKANUAK* IS "THOSE WHO MIGRATED TO AMERICA OF BASQUE DESCENT." Generally, these were first-generation immigrants who risked migration from their homeland for various social, political, and economic reasons to build better lives for themselves and their families in America. These immigrants predominately focused inward on their own ethnic group to help ensure a successful transition to American life. Amerikanuak adapted to external Americanization pressures throughout this era, and their given natal identity was manifested differently through time and place.

Beginning in the late nineteenth century and continuing into the early twentieth centuries, an astounding number of white Europeans migrated to the United States. Between 1880 and 1920, more than twenty-three million immigrants had entered the nation's ports of entry.[1] By the end of the 1920s, almost a quarter of the white American population included those who had been born to immigrant parents.[2] Amerikanuak joined many other Europeans who also searched for improved fortune beyond their birthplace countries.

The sheep industry of the American West became a primary employer of Basque men who chose to come to America. Most Basques were willing to work in the high desert mountains as sheepherders for a good part of the year a seasonal labor force.[3] Although the jobs were physically and emotionally challenging due to harsh outdoor conditions, strenuous physical demands, and isolation from humans for long periods of time, Basques filled those positions with hopes of economic prosperity.

LEKUAK: THE BASQUE PLACES OF BOISE, IDAHO

The 1900 U.S. Census counted 986 Basques, which was likely a low number because they were often counted as Spanish or French immigrants.[4] By 1910, the U.S. Census showed that Basque numbers had swelled to 8,398 migrants in the states of California, Nevada, Idaho, and Wyoming, probably still an underrepresented tally due to misidentification of Basques as a unique ethnic group.[5] That same year, 999 Basques were recorded in Idaho.[6] In Boise, Basques joined other European ethnic groups such as the Irish, Germans, Italians, and Greeks.[7]

Most of the Amerikanuak came from the rural countryside and fishing villages of the Basque Country. The first Basques were mostly men, but women soon followed the migration pattern, some even making the journey alone. The Amerikanuak had limited education, were usually unable to speak English, and rarely integrated with larger American culture. They primarily expressed their ethnicity as an internally-focused, solely-Basque ethnic group, and in their later years, almost always married within their ethnic group.

Amerikanuak places in Boise supported economic and social survival, including basic human needs: shelter, food, and community. Immigrants were often separated from the larger American society that was undergoing an influx of new arrivals who were assuming the role of a lower-class labor force. Amerikanuak places, therefore, were almost always solely Basque, with the purpose of meeting communal needs of a cohesive ethnic group.

Immigrants constructed diverse ethnic communities during the nineteenth and early twentieth centuries by transplanting unique homeland traditions to their new places in America, which helped them transition to American ways of life.[8] In Boise, the Basques constructed community based on their homeland traditions, which resulted in a Basque enclave on Grove Street near downtown. Greeks, Irish, Jewish, Germans, and Chinese formed similar ethnic enclaves in the city.[9]

Many European immigrants, including Basques, sailed across the Atlantic in steamships and then were processed into the United States at Ellis Island in New York. Photos courtesy museumsyndicates.com.

AMERIKANUAK

Irish historian Paddy Woodworth noted that ethnic groups were "often deeply dependent on memories of the homeland to nurture their sense of identity and self-worth."[10] The role of homeland memory was vital to the establishment of immigrant group communities. Memory of homeland, coupled with shared language and customs, assisted the first generation because it provided a foundation for operating within shared experiences of the ethnic group. Dependence on homeland memory also had the potential of isolating some members of the immigrant group from broader society.

AMERIKANUAK PLACES

Amerikanuak places in Boise included boardinghouses, frontons (pelota courts for Basque handball), and the nation's only Basque church, Boise's Church of the Good Shepherd. Most of these Amerikanuak places were not reconstructions of homeland places, however. They were largely American forms with Basque culture superimposed over existing structures. For instance, Basque boardinghouses were often repurposed dwellings that housed both boarders and Basque proprietor's families. Basques did not build their own ethnic churches. Boise's Good Shepherd Church was comprised of existing secular buildings that were sold to the Catholic Church in 1911 to meet the needs of a fast-growing Basque community. Frontons, however, were distinctively Basque places that were reconstructed from homeland memory. Frontons almost always were connected to the boardinghouses in America; they were usually in close proximity to these establishments. This was a departure from the frontons that were usually attached to churches as a central part of Basque Country village plazas.

AMERIKANUAK

Places by Basques, for Basques (Late 1800s-1920s)

- Boardinghouses
- Frontons
- Churches

The Church of the Good Shepherd

The Anduiza boardinghouse and fronton was built in 1914 on Grove Street, intended to provide a place of lodging and recreation to Basque immigrants. Photo by "Boise by Burns" photography; courtesy Basque Museum and Cultural Center, Boise, Idaho.

LEKUAK: THE BASQUE PLACES OF BOISE, IDAHO

All of the Amerikanuak places were created by Basques for Basques, and express Jean Phinney's first stage of "given identity," with preassigned ethnic identity from birth that produced strong natal ties to homeland language, values, and customs.[11] This resulted in an internally focused, communal monoculture that did not assimilate rapidly into the larger American society. This concept becomes apparent as the Amerikanuak evolved through time, which influenced both the development of immigrants' given identities and their places. Boardinghouses reflect the Amerikanuak identity that begins as a strong attachment to the collective ethnic group.

Boardinghouses

The Basque ancestral house, or *etxea*, was the "the root and the axis around which life revolved."[12] The etxea was the most important place in traditional society, as it guaranteed the social and economic self-sufficiency of the larger community.[13] Woodworth wrote that the Basque etxea was transplanted to the United States, with both those who were *baserritarrak* (from a village's rural farmhouse or *baserri*), and the *kaletarrak* (literally "from the streets," or more urban cities or coastal villages).

Faced with an uncertain future, Amerikanuak largely stayed together, beginning with their train trip across the country and continuing when they settled in western towns. Immigrants usually first arrived at a boardinghouse, or an *ostatua*. This central gathering spot was a communal place where Basques lived and socialized, with familiar values, language, food, and cultural customs that could be shared with other Basque immigrants. It also was where many Basques met their future spouses. The boardinghouse was a place that accommodated the given identity of the ethnic group, as it reinforced the internal cultural circle in almost all aspects of life. The boardinghouse was the primary ethnic place in the cultural landscape of the American West, a unique creation of Basque settlement. It played a central role in the social, economic, and emotional survival of the first-generation immigrants. It was etxea: the place of home.

Amerikanuak often arrived by train after a long journey west from New York. Early boardinghouses in Boise were located near the Oregon Short Line train station (photo c. 1895). Photo courtesy Basque Museum and Cultural Center, Boise, Idaho.

AMERIKANUAK

Jeronima Echeverria's seminal work on Basque boardinghouses, *Home Away from Home*, credits the institution with a primary role in the preservation of Basque culture.[14] Echeverria recounted stories about some of the "tens of thousands of Basques who immigrated to the United States between the years of 1890 and 1930. During those years, the *ostatuak* (boardinghouses) became the most important social and ethnic institutions in the lives of new Basque immigrants."[15] The boardinghouse network also led to the development of the first Basque ethnic enclaves in the western states of Idaho, Nevada, Wyoming, and California.[16] Boise's boardinghouse network was extensive: fifty-two boardinghouses operated between the late 1800s and the 1970s, peaking in the late 1920s and early 1930s.[17]

Felipe and Maria Josefa Azpiri Aldape operated the Eagle Hotel in Boise. Photo courtesy Basque Museum and Cultural Center, Boise, Idaho.

The boardinghouse was a purely American Basque institution, created by first-generation Basque immigrants. There were no Basque boardinghouses in Euskal Herria, but the Basques transferred the concept of the etxea as the core of society, the center of family, and source of economic self-sufficiency to the boardinghouse of the American West.

Amerikanuak were committed to the traditional principle of auzolan. This was evident when Basques helped one another with securing employment, finding places to live, communicating with non-Basques, and raising families. The story of Maria Josefa Azpiri illustrates the principle of auzolan, from her first experiences in America to her family's tradition of operating boardinghouses in Boise. Maria boarded *La Lorraine*, a trans-Atlantic steamer, on September 10, 1910, in response to her father's request to join him in America. José Mari Azpiri was a foreman on the dynamite crew at Arrowrock Dam near Boise who wanted his daughter near him. Maria crossed an ocean, lost her luggage, and saw a banana for the first time. Her travel was arranged by Basques who helped her navigate the journey from Euskal Herria to New York, and then on to Boise. She spent her first night in America with other Basques at Valentin Aguirre's New York boardinghouse. Aguirre then arranged her five-day journey by train to Boise, Idaho. When Maria arrived in Boise, she was met at the train station by Basques who had been contacted by Aguirre from New York, who helped her walk to her new "home away from home" at Mateo Arregui's boardinghouse. There, she rolled up her sleeves and got to cooking and cleaning as a maid, a job that had been arranged for her.[18] Maria's entire immigration experience was a product of auzolan, the Basque commitment to communal work for the greater group.

A dashing young Basque sheepherder, Felipe Aldape, who was staying at Arregui's boardinghouse on a break, caught Maria's eye. Maria and Felipe married in 1911. On their wedding night, Maria slipped out of her beautiful wedding gown and into working clothes so that she could return to scrubbing boardinghouse floors. Boardinghouse operations became a way of life for the couple, as did many Basque couples who built lives in Boise. Eventually they operated the Eagle Hotel at 910 Grove Street from 1929 to 1931. The Aldape's daughter Angeles and her husband Justo Murelaga later continued the family boardinghouse tradition with they opened Economy Rooms in 1936.[19] The boardinghouse networks were forms of auzolan, and most maintained close internal ethnic connections solely within the Basques, some even into the second generations.

Mateo and Adriana Arregui at their Modern Rooming House at 613 1/2 Idaho Street. Photo courtesy Basque Museum and Cultural Center, Boise, Idaho.

Boardinghouses were the first permanent places of this ethnic group, although the lives of their inhabitants were almost also transitional and temporary. Boardinghouses were often re-purposed structures such as old hotels or homes, not new construction. Families usually lived with the boarders in the boardinghouses, too. Boardinghouses served many purposes for immigrants, and they were essential to the survival of the Amerikanuak generation. These Basque places were symbols of ethnic expression that impacted the cultural landscape for many years. Of fifty-two documented boardinghouses that operated in Boise from the late 1800s to the mid-1970s, six still survive as icons of Basque communal living:[20]

AMERIKANUAK

- *Anduiza Hotel and Fronton*: 619 Grove Street; operated by Juan and Juana Gabiola Anduiza from 1914–1945.

- *Arriola's/Saracondi's:* 211 South Sixth St.; Juan and Juana Arriola Uberuaga, 1909; also appears in records 1917 to 1921.

- *Belaustegui's:* The first was at 117. South 7th; Augustin and Francesco "Patxa" Balaustegui, from 1918 to 1935; later opened at 117 South Sixth; a boardinghouse with the addition of the Chico Club which the family operated until 1957.

Antonio Letemendi operated several boardinghouses in Boise. Photo courtesy Basque Museum and Cultural Center, Boise, Idaho.

- *Star Lodging House:* José and Felipa Garrechena Uberuaga operated from 1906–1913 at 512 West Idaho St.; later named Star Rooming House, operated by Francisco and Gabina Goitia Aguirre from c. 1915–1972 at the same location.

- *Uberuaga's*: 607 Grove Street; previously operated by Simon and Josepha Alegria Galdos in 1910, followed by Ciriaco and Mari Cruz Bicandi, and finally, José and Hermegilda Uberuaga rented it from 1917 to 1928 when they purchased it and operated until 1969. (This was the former Cyrus Jacobs home, built in 1864.)

- *Valencia Hotel and Restaurant:* 620 W. Idaho Street; Two families joined together to create this Basque boardinghouse that sought to also cater to the non-Basque community. Brothers Benito and Tomas Ysursa and their wives, Asuncion and Antonia respectively, continued their partnership from the previous boardinghouse known as the Modern Hotel. Their two- story establishment across the street had traditional boarding on the first floor, and a full-service restaurant on the second floor: open to the public. Management passed to Ramon Ysursa (son of Benito and Asuncion) and wife Begona, and then to cousin Emeterio Ysursa and his wife Adela. The final managers were Juan Uscola and Cristina Ormaetxea (sister of Begona) before the building was sold when the boarding house era came to a close in the 1970s.

LEKUAK: THE BASQUE PLACES OF BOISE, IDAHO

Most Basques of the Amerikanuak generation lived primarily within their tight ethnic group circle. They usually socialized with other Basques, spoke Euskara, and maintained their food and other cultural customs in the boardinghouses. The boardinghouses were instruments of cultural community that were fundamental to the establishment and maintenance of ethnic enclaves. Echeverria's claim that "Basque *ostatuak* were key to establishing what is today a still-thriving Basque colony in southern Idaho [Boise]" is validated by the fact that over a hundred years ago, these internally focused institutions provided critical social and economic stability for the Amerikanuak.

Amerikanuak relied on their given identity to maintain a cohesive ethnic group amid the larger forces of Americanization. Basque places such as boardinghouses reflected the retention of given ethnic identity. The places that remained represent the persistence of Basques during a period of immigration and assimilation into American society.[21] This "home away from home" was also a place where the principle of auzolan supported economic and social needs: it was the etxea of the New World. The boardinghouse ensured community cohesion and continuity of cultural tradition, especially with shared language, food, dance, and music. Unmistakably rooted in Old World tradition, these ethnic places enabled the initial Basque settlement of Boise.

Frontons

The Basque handball court, or *fronton* (also called a *pelota/pilota* court), was another communal place of the Amerikanuak generation. It was the only distinctively Basque structure that was transplanted from the Old Country to the American West. These handball courts were usually open-air, single or double-walled, usually adjacent to the church or plaza. For centuries Basque frontons were central communal places where the whole village watched players compete in fast and rigorous handball games. The stronger men played *esku pelota* with their bare hands. The game became *pala* if paddles were used.

In the United States, the fronton joined the boardinghouse and the church as Amerikanuak gathering places where Basques could share time with one another and compete in their national sport.[22] At least four frontons were built in Boise between 1910 and 1914 by the Amerikanuak generation. Frontons later introduced non-Basques to Basque culture, when outside spectators could watch the handball games being played in communities where they lived.

AMERIKANUAK

The *Idaho Statesman* published a news story in 1915 about a pala game at the Anduiza Fronton, "Shouts and hurrahs coming from the vicinity of Sixth and Grove streets caused some conjecture as to what might be the matter Friday afternoon. It is an odd game played in a walled court, the ball is batted about with small paddles."[23]

Boise Basque Henry Alegria documented Boise's frontons in his book *75 Years of Memoirs*. Domingo Zabala built Boise's first fronton in 1910 at 631 Lovers Lane, (near today's River and Ash Streets). Zabala borrowed $1000 ($25,700 in 2017 dollars) from fellow Basque José Eiguren to build a small court.[24] Eiguren purchased the fronton from Zabala in 1913. As was the tradition with many Amerikanuak, Basques often kept business within their own ethnic circles, so another Basque, Manuel Aberasturi finally operated the fronton from 1914 until 1915.[25] The fronton walls eventually evolved into the walls of Marcelino Arana's Basque Bakery.[26]

Archaeologist Pam Demo's "South Side of the Tracks" study focused on the River Street neighborhood near the railroad, where the Zabala fronton existed. Demo's research revealed Basque names such as Bicandi, Alegria, Bastida, and Aberasturi, members of Boise's Basque community who gathered at this neighborhood fronton to play handball.[27] Demo also documented other ethnic groups that lived in this multi-ethnic neighborhood of Basques, African-Americans, Austrians, and Croatians, which opened a new area of ethnic study for Boise.

Basques moved away from River and Ash, as did many of the remaining ethnic groups, and city progress obliterated the fronton and the bakery site. Evidence of the River Street fronton had been lost forever to city development, covered by years of asphalt, soil, and grass.

Idaho Statesman photo of players at the Anduiza fronton. Basque players Henry Alegria and Stack Yribar. Photos courtesy Basque Museum and Cultural Center, Boise, Idaho, and Henry Alegria, 75 Years of Memoirs.

LEKUAK: THE BASQUE PLACES OF BOISE, IDAHO

Archaeologist Bill White's *River Street Archaeology Project* during the summer of 2015, however, rediscovered Boise's ethnic past when he and his team of archaeology students uncovered remnants of the Zabala fronton in an archaeological dig. White triumphed about the significant historical discovery of this marker of Basque cultural persistence:

> We found the earliest Basque handball court in Boise, something historians believed was lost. This solidified the character of our work as truly multiethnic and bigger than a simple discussion of African Americans in the West. It also allowed the sizeable Basque community to connect with a project they may have not been otherwise interested.[28]

The second Basque fronton in Boise was built in 1910 by Basque pioneers and brothers Antonio and Augustin Azcuenaga, and their close friends José Navarro and Pedro Arritola.[29] This fronton was attached to the west side of the three-story Hotel Iberia at 213 South 9th (later the Oregon Hotel) across from the train station.[30] It is not known whether the addition of the fronton was intended to draw more Basques to the Azcuenaga boardinghouse, or whether it was intended to serve a larger communal need, but the new fronton was a curiosity to those not in Basque culture. An *Idaho Statesman* story described the Hotel Iberia fronton in December of 1910 from an outsider perspective:

> The mystery of the Bastille-like walls which have recently been erected at the rear of the Hotel Iberia, which have aroused the curiosity of many passersby, has been solved through an interview with A.B. Azcuenaga of the Hotel Iberia who stated that the frowning gray walls which tower to a height of 50 feet on two sides of the lot at the rear of the hotel were not built with a prison, but for sheer pleasure, in order to enable the natives of sunny Spain and the province of Basque, who are now living in Boise, to indulge in their national game of ball. The court is filled with players from morning until dusk each day. It cost the sum of $1000.[31]

A year after the Azcuenaga fronton was erected, and not far from 9th Street, José and Felipa Garrechena Uberuaga built another outdoor fronton on the west side of their Star boardinghouse at 512 West Idaho Street. It is possible José Uberuaga, known as *Arotxa* or "the carpenter," an avid pelota and pala player, built the fronton himself. This fronton was unique because it also had a canopy that protected the players from the weather, which drew many more players to the spot. Gabina Goitia Aguirre and her husband Francisco, ("Frank," also known as "Zapatero" (shoemaker) for his shoe store and repair skills), managed the Star from 1915 through 1974. One remnant wall of the fronton still stands as of 2017. Although this was predominately a place of given Basque ethnic identity for the Basques, the

AMERIKANUAK

Star fronton attracted Boiseans of various ethnic backgrounds who watched the traditional sport. The Star fronton remnant remains a visible record of the cultural persistence of Basques today.[32]

"Big Jack" and Juana Anduiza built a new boardinghouse at 619 Grove Street in 1914. Big Jack also constructed the city's largest and only indoor public fronton, attached directly to the boardinghouse. The *Idaho Statesman* reported on this Basque place on Grove Street:

> A building, probably unique in the West, has been commenced on the south side of Grove Street between Sixth and Seventh, where Juan Anduiza is putting up a rooming house enclosing a handball court. The court will be 28 feet wide and 122 feet long. Opening directly on the court will be sleeping rooms, a dining room, and a kitchen. On the street grade, the building will have 11 rooms. These will open on a wide balcony which overlooks the court.[33]

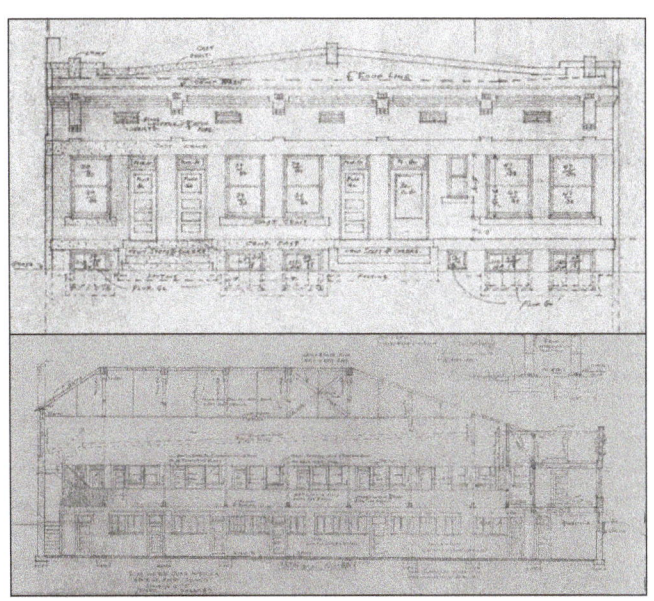

Anduiza boardinghouse and fronton blueprints; The Anduiza family; Antonio Azcuenaga and José Navarro at their Hotel Iberia and fronton. Photos courtesy Basque Museum and Cultural Center, Boise, Idaho.

LEKUAK: THE BASQUE PLACES OF BOISE, IDAHO

Anduiza's handball competitions also included betting with cash prizes, which netted more spectators than at the outdoor fronton games where there was no betting.[34]

Known for his intense competitive demeanor, Anduiza set up thousands of Basque handball competitions, often between towns such as Mountain Home and Boise. Anduiza's fronton was spectacular, and generations of Basques played and watched competitions there, cementing it as a Basque communal place until 1945 when Anduizas sold the building. The building was subsumed by American assimilation, when it was transferred into the hands of the U.S. Department of Veterans' Affairs, and then later to the Briggs family engineering firm until 1972.[35]

Some argue that the Basques did not leave a notable ethnic mark on the American landscape. Basque frontons, however, were distinctly communal places that originated in the homeland and were usually constructed within internal Amerikanuak internal enclaves. They were closely associated with the Basque boardinghouses in America.[36]

Anduiza's boardinghouse and fronton is an example of an internally focused, Basque-only place, but it grew to be a public spot where some non-Basques became interested in the Basque sport and supported the games. The Anduiza Fronton left a visible trace of ethnicity on the Boise landscape. It remains as the oldest standing indoor fronton in the United States today, and it is one of two covered frontons in the American West that still stand (the San Francisco Basque Cultural Center built their indoor fronton in 1982.)[37]

Anduiza fronton court. Photos by 'Boise by Burns' photography; courtesy Basque Museum and Cultural Center, Boise, Idaho.

AMERIKANUAK

The fronton was an extension of communal living space, an integral part of social sustenance and cultural maintenance. The frontons of the Amerikanuak generation were initially used only by Basques, which mirrored the response of many immigrant cultures to greater American society to first operate within their own ethnic enclave. Frontons stand as a symbol of both Old and New World Basque ethnic tradition, and they paved the way for the integration of Basque sport with American culture.

Frontons were Amerikanuak places that represented the first-generation transplantation of their national sport, a homeland tradition, in form and function to American soil. Initially internally focused, they align with social theory that first-generation ethnics retained their given identity, even after immigration to a new host country. As Basque immigrants asserted their homeland sport within the larger American culture, they both enclosed themselves within their own ethnic group as members who knew the sport, and they also exposed their ethnic uniqueness to non-Basques who watched the game. The fronton was the only distinctively Basque place that was transplanted from the Old Country to America, and it retained its form and function in the Amerikanuak era until the Basque boardinghouses declined. In fact, the reclamation and active use today of the Anduiza Fronton by contemporary handball leagues underscores the persistence of Basque culture on the modern landscape.

Players still use the Anduiza fronton in Boise today, including competitive league games. Photo courtesy John Bieter.

LEKUAK: THE BASQUE PLACES OF BOISE, IDAHO

Churches: *The Church of the Good Shepherd*

Religion was integral to Basque culture and identity, and the Amerikanuak transferred that value to their new country. Similar to other immigrants such as the Irish, Italians, Polish, Jews and Orthodox Russians, this practice reinforced the internal structure of the ethnic groups. Susan Hardwick noted this in her study of Russians who settled in California's Sacramento Valley during the early twentieth century, "Religious connections forge strong ties among immigrants and their families, and emotional bonds within religious groups intensify as individuals struggle to establish their new lives in an often challenging new place."[38] Basque religious connections in America helped to establish and maintain strong cultural ties among the immigrants, and their religious practices often stabilized the ethnic enclaves by gathering immigrants tighter into their own circles. Religion for the first-generation immigrant was a social unifier, which was a manifestation of first-generation given identity.

In the Old Country, almost every Basque village had a church. Usually the focal place in the village plaza, the church was possibly one of the most important social places of the Basque Country.[39] The church was also a significant place for the Basques in America. When young immigrant Florencio "Pancho" Aldape arrived in Boise he recalled, "I assumed the Capitol building was the church, since in Euskadi the biggest building was always the church."[40]

First Communion Class at the Church of the Good Shepherd, c. 1919-1921. Photo courtesy Basque Museum and Cultural Center, Boise, Idaho.

AMERIKANUAK

In the early Amerikanuak era, St. John's was the primary Catholic parish. In 1910, the Basque population was expanding rapidly, and the church needed extra support to administer to this growing congregation.[41] That year, thirty-eight Basque marriages had been performed in Boise, but language posed a communication and record-keeping issue for both the Basques and the priests who could not speak Euskara.[42]

There was the perception that Basque immigrants were clannish and not integrated into American society, however. Carmelo Urza noted that the Basques of this era were perceived to be "on the margins of society ... generally isolated as a group, who kept to their own kind, and no one knew or cared too much about them."[43]

Bishop Alphonse J. Glorieux knew about the Basques though, and he did not want to risk losing these European Catholics. He recognized that language was a primary issue for the Basque congregation, so he arranged for a Basque priest to come to Boise to administer to the Basque "foreign-born flock":[44]

> Eventually the high tide of foreign immigration overflowed from the eastern seaboard to distant Idaho. Numerous Basque people entered the wide sheep ranges of southern Idaho and several colonies of Italians followed the railroads. They were Catholics in their homelands, and the possible loss of their faith in a foreign land, whose language they knew not, gravely troubled the apostolic Bishop. He arranged with the Bishop of Vitoria, Spain for the services of a Basque priest, Rev. Bernardo Arregui, who arrived in Boise, July 11, 1911.[45]

The Church of the Good Shepherd's Basque priest, Father (Aita) Arregui. Photo courtesy Basque Museum and Cultural Center, Boise, Idaho.

LEKUAK: THE BASQUE PLACES OF BOISE, IDAHO

When Father Arregui was assigned to the Basques that summer, his native language of Euskara became an immediate connection among the Amerikanuak parishioners, both for prayer and fraternity. The Basques gathered as a cohesive ethnic group to support one another during this period, which reinforced their internal, monocultural lifestyle, and in turn, may have slowed the assimilation process.

The Basque Catholic community grew even more between 1911 and 1919, and church records show the Basque priest from Tolosa was stretched thin, both with his Basque congregation and with his travel to a large geographic area that extended beyond Boise.[46] Between August and December of 1911, Father Arregui conducted fourteen Basque marriages in Boise alone, not including the towns outside the city he was traveling to for weddings, baptisms, First Communions, and burials. Bishop Glorieux's replacement, Bishop Daniel M. Gorman, decided that the answer to accommodating the large number of Basques in Boise was to seek approval for a solely Basque church near Boise's Basque boardinghouses and frontons where most of this ethnic group lived and worked. City Councilman Thomas Finnegan sold two buildings at Fifth and Idaho Streets to the Catholic Church in Boise: one for a church and another for the parish rectory for $18,000 ($463,000 in 2017 dollars).[47]

On March 2, 1919, Bishop Gorman blessed the Church of the Good Shepherd at 422 West Idaho Street, the only Basque church in the United States. Father Bernardo Arregui delivered the homily in Euskara to a capacity congregation of about a hundred attendees. Arregui drew connections between the old Basque Country and the Basques' new U.S. homeland, as he reminded his Basque parishioners that this place was "an ornament to this hospitable city in which you live and to which you owe so much, and a joy and satisfaction to your parents who live on the other side of the broad Atlantic ... the church will be an inestimable inheritance for your children."[48] This statement indicated that the concept of place was central even from the religious perspective, and that the church represented primary Basque values on both sides of the Atlantic. Yet, Father Arregui's message was representative of the Amerikanuak ethnic expression: it was internal, focused on Basque given identity, and tied to the motherland.

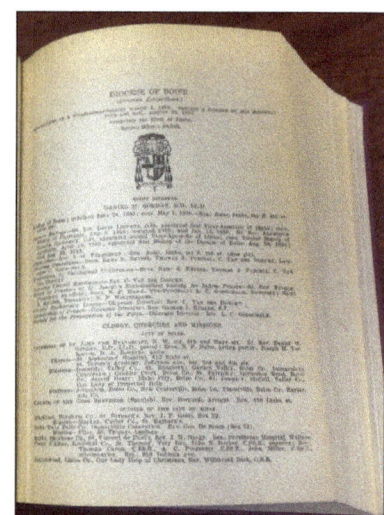

The Church of the Good Shepherd and Rev. Arregui in Diocesan records. Courtesy Catholic Diocese of Boise, Idaho.

AMERIKANUAK

On March 19, 1919, Candido Aboritz Arrutia from the Basque town of Gabica Ereño, and Ygnacio Azqueta Ysasi from Gernika were the first Basque couple to be married by Father Arregui at the newly established ethnic church, followed by forty-three more in the little church until 1921.[49] Including the years before the Church of the Good Shepherd existed, Father Arregui also had presided over 196 Basque burials in Boise up to 1921.[50] The records certainly support the assertion that the church was also a primary place for the Amerikanuak in Boise.

By 1921 a larger societal phenomenon was occurring, however. The country was becoming fearful of immigrants from ethnic groups who had entered the United States, and a movement to exclude them from entering, working, or praying in America emerged. The Amerikanuak generation witnessed the "closing of the gates" to immigrants. The anti-immigrant sentiment had begun a few years previous, when restrictive congressional legislation in 1917 required literacy tests for all immigrants over the age of sixteen, and imposed immigration quotas largely due to xenophobic fears of the World War I period, the patriotic Red Scare, and the belief that ethnic groups posed harm to American society.[51]

The Emergency Quota Act of 1921 was aimed at preserving homogeneity in the country.[52] Accordingly, American Catholic Church leaders followed a new policy of integrating ethnic parishes into the larger "American Church." In an effort to display loyalty only to the United States of America, church leaders closed all ethnic churches, and followed the announcements with indications that there was also a fiscal need to consolidate.[53] This action led to the "abrupt end of the Church of the Good Shepherd as a Basque chapel. Its closure dealt a blow to the Basque community."[54] Father (Aita) Arregui, the beloved Basque priest who had been such a part of Boise's Basque cultural community for just over ten years, was relocated to Twin Falls. From 1921 to 1928, St. John's Cathedral reduced weekly Mass to only once a week, but not in Euskara, and not solely for the Basques. The ethnic church's doors had been officially closed and primary attendance for Basque Catholics (as American Catholics) was directed to St. John's Cathedral.[55]

The Church of the Good Shepherd could not stand up to the larger American cultural shift that gained momentum after 1921. The Immigration Act of 1924, also known as the Johnson-Reed Act, limited the number of immigrants to the United States, which further restricted the legal entry of many Basques into the country.[56] Under the 1921 Emergency Quota Act, Spanish immigration was limited to 912 persons per year; the 1924 Act reduced that to 131 annually, which prompted the Bieters to declare that this law "ended Basques' large-scale entry into the American West — or at least their legal entry."[57]

LEKUAK: THE BASQUE PLACES OF BOISE, IDAHO

This was just the tip of the iceberg, as prejudice and suspicion of ethnic groups besides Basques also increased, just as it did against the Chinese and Germans. The impact of ethnic suspicion and the pressure on immigrants to be "American" also brought a close to a primary Amerikanuak place: the Church of the Good Shepherd. The Church of the Good Shepherd, the only Basque church in America, was an example of the Amerikanuak generation's given identity that was expressed in an internally focused manner, although it only existed for a short time.[58]

Conclusion

The Amerikanuak reflect Phinney's sociological model of ethnic identity development. In the first phase, "given identity," the first generation's preassigned ethnic identity from birth is predominant. This produces an internal, communal monoculture that does not easily assimilate into larger society.[59] The Amerikanuak might well have largely stayed with their given identity if not for external pressures of Americanization. The places of the Amerikanuak were mostly created by Basques, for Basques. The Basque principle of auzolan guided Amerikanuak migration, settlement, and place development.

This internal dynamic of communal work was not the sole determinant, however, as Amerikanuak were faced with external challenges in America of the 1920s. These pressured the Amerikanuak to move out of their internal ethnic groups and into assimilation. Here we see the power of both time and place.

This era produced powerful economic and political determinants, influencing the "push" factors of assimilation. The 1929 stock market crash and the Depression brought the sheep industry to its knees with declining lamb and wool prices. The Taylor Grazing Act of 1934 restricted economic opportunities in the sheep industry for the Amerikanuak even more.[60]

Sheepcamp. Photo courtesy University of Nevada, Reno, Center for Basque Studies. Sheepherder in Idaho. Photo by Boise by Burns photography; courtesy Basque Museum and Cultural Center, Boise, Idaho.

AMERIKANUAK

This, coupled with the intense scrutiny on immigrants forever changed the economic, social, and political outlook in the American West for the first generation immigrant.

The Amerikanuak's boardinghouses, frontons, and the short-lived Church of the Good Shepherd were places of physical, economic, and social survival. They were places of natal ethnic identity. The boardinghouse provided a "home away from home" to herders and Basques new to the United States, but also they were portals of integration. The fronton was an extension of communal living space, initially only used by Basques. We will see later in the Egungoak generation how the re-purposed fronton paved the way for the integration of Basque sport with American culture. Finally, the Church of the Good Shepherd embodies the response to segregate this ethnic group as a separate entity, and its closure reflected the emphasis of that era on an American "melting pot," even with regards to religion.

By the 1930s, rather than looking inward within their own cultural community to survive, Basques demonstrated adaptability, and slipped into the Tartekoak period of dual American and Basque culture, upward mobility, and wartime assimilation.

Larry Arguinchona and Julia Luque Laraway at the Delamar boardinghouse. Photo courtesy Julia Luque Laraway, through Basque Museum and Cultural Center, Boise, Idaho.

CHAPTER 2 – BI
TARTEKOAK

Vince's Barbershop, Boise, Idaho. Original photo courtesy Vincente Echeverria Facebook page. Digital photo illustration by Meggan Laxalt Mackey.

Dominique and Thérèse Alpetche Laxalt's six Tartekoak generation children. Photo courtesy Laxalt Family.

CHAPTER 2 – BI ‖ TARTEKOAK
Bridges between Two Worlds (1930s – 1950s)

*All of us together were of a generation born of old country people
who spoke English with an accent and prayed in another language,
who drank red wine and cooked their food in the old country way,
and peeled apples and pears after dinner.*

*We were among the last whose names would tell our blood
and the kind of faces we had, to know another language in our homes,
to suffer youthful shame because of that language and refuse to speak it,
and a later shame because of what we had done, and hurt
because we had caused a hurt so deep it could never find words.*

*And the irony of it was that our mothers and fathers were truer
Americans than we, because they had forsaken home and family, and gone into
the unknown of a new land with only courage and the hands that God gave them,
and had given us in our turn the right to be born American. And in a little while,
even our sons would forget, and the old country people would be
only a dimming memory, and names would mean nothing,
and the melting would be done.*

Robert Laxalt, *Sweet Promised Land*

LEKUAK: THE BASQUE PLACES OF BOISE, IDAHO

Tartekoak children were raised in dual worlds: Basque and American. Photo courtesy Laxalt Family.

TARTEKOAK

THE BASQUE TRANSLATION OF *TARTEKOAK* IS "BETWEEN" OR "INTERMEDIATE." These children of immigrant parents grappled with what it meant be Basque, American, and finally, a "hyphenated" Basque-American. Tartekoak found themselves bridging gaps between two cultures, which almost always left them questioning whether to align with their parents' birthright Basque ethnicity, or, if they were born in the United States, their American citizenship. Tartekoak with dual identity generally expressed their Basque heritage privately at home or in their internal ethnic circles, and then publicly expressed their claim to "being American." John and Mark Bieter noted that these second-generation Basques were very much straddling both American and Basque worlds:

> They had grown up in Basque homes, speaking Basque, hearing Basque music, eating Basque food, but their years in American schools, American neighborhoods, and American churches changed them . . . by the 1930s, most second-generation Basques consciously — or not — had moved into the almost irreversible pattern of American living.[1]

A gap exists in the establishment of Basque places between the 1930s and the late 1940s, more than half of this era. This was a transition period when some of the larger American society had become wary of the foreign-born, and immigrant loyalty to the United States was questioned. This placed pressure on the Tartekoak generation to demonstrate their allegiance to America, not to their immigrant Amerikanuak parents' places of birth.

Despite being descendants of an ethnic group that had once been targeted for obliteration by oppressive leaders such as Franco in the Basque Country, many Basques during this period deemphasized their Basqueness in favor of open displays of Americanization. World War II also united Basque-Americans in war efforts. Some Basque men served in the war, and others, such as the Basque Company of the Ada County Volunteers, supported the war with public display of their American patriotism in public halls, parades, and humanitarian efforts.[2]

"Being Basque" and "Being American" presented challenges to the Tartekoak generation. Boise Basque Company, Ada County Volunteers, 1942. Photo courtesy Basque Museum and Cultural Center.

LEKUAK: THE BASQUE PLACES OF BOISE, IDAHO

As Amerikanuak Basques merged into World War II society where the primary goal was to be American, Tartekoak spoke English publicly, played baseball instead of pelota, and ate hamburgers rather than lamb or solomo. Eustaquio Garroguerricaechevarria was transformed into "Ed Garro," and Tartekoak children carried baptismal names such as Anthony or Mary, not Andoni or Maite.[3] These were open declarations of American allegiance. Yet, the Tartekoak were Basque by blood and of foreign-born parentage. This generation's expression of ethnic duality deeply influenced the dearth of solely Basque places during this era. Tartekoak places represented the evolution of Basques into Basque-Americans, with little outward evidence of one's ethnic heritage.

Tartekoak often revealed individuation from their immigrant Basque parents' homes and other ethnic places. The majority moved away from the ethnic boardinghouse neighborhoods and to the suburbs, where owning a private single-dwelling residence demonstrated an American goal. This was a watershed development for the Tartekoak, a huge step beyond the previous generation's lower-class communal living patterns, and a jump toward assimilated American society.

Basque Women's Auxiliary c. 1933. Virginia Mingo Shelley and Benita Mingo Schaffner. Photos courtesy Basque Museum and Cultural Center.

TARTEKOAK PLACES

Economic, geographic, and educational mobility were key to this period. Access to education separated families geographically, especially compared to the homeland where it was rare to travel even twenty miles from one's birthplace. This new mobility in America encouraged Basque dispersion due to education, employment, and even marriage. Tartekoak were given opportunities to study outside their city, state, and sometimes, nation. Intermarriage also encouraged Basque mobility during this period, which accelerated the process of assimilation for those who moved outside their ethnic circle to other places.

One study of Basque marriage patterns concluded that although most first-generation Basques did not intermarry, the second generation married non-Basques by a six to four ratio.[4]

Because Tartekoak were usually proficient in English, they acquired jobs beyond the previous Amerikanuak labor-oriented occupations that demanded little in terms of language or education. As Tartekoak gained degrees, professional experiences, and specialized skills, they became more socially accepted into American businesses, sports, churches, and the military. As they were elevated above the immigrant working class, some Basques became respected community members, elected officials, businesspeople, and professionals. This elevated the status of Tartekoak socially and economically. Basques worked frequently within the American mainstream, but some formed their own independent businesses and workplaces during the Tartekoak period. Conversely, older-generation Amerikanuak places began to fade.

The frontons grew silent, as Basque handball lost to the popularity of American sports. *Boise Capital News* reported in 1937, "The two courts [Basque handball courts] don't ring with the shouts of young Basques engaged in competition. The new Basques like the gridiron, the basketball court, and the baseball diamond."[5]

Boise's Church of the Good Shepherd closed, its Basque priest transferred out of Boise, and many members of the all-Basque congregation became entrenched in St. John's Cathedral or other local American parishes. Tartekoak were the first generation to bury a large number of fellow Basques on American soil. The value of religion remained strong with

TARTEKOAK
Bridges between Two Worlds (1930s - 1950s)

- **Residences**

- **Workplaces**

- **Morris Hill Cemetery**
  St. John's Section

- **Residences**

- **Temporary Places**
  Picnics and Mutual Aid Society Events

- **Boise's Basque Center**

Vince's Barbershop was a city mainstay for years. Photo courtesy Vincente Echeverria Facebook page.

the second generation, and most chose to have Catholic funerals followed by burials in the St. John's Catholic section of the Morris Hill Cemetery. The cemetery remained one Basque place that demonstrated ethnic expression as a separate group, visibly marked by headstones.

Tartekoak retained their desire to gather communally after the Amerikanuak boardinghouses had declined and most Basques had moved to single-family dwellings. They resorted to temporary gathering places such as parks and rented social halls to serve the need for communal social activity within the ethnic group. It would not be until the last years of the Tartekoak period (1948–1950), however, that a solely Basque place for communal gathering was created: Boise's Basque Center.

As this generation approached the cusp of the 1950s, an impending social shift among the Tartekoak occurred, due to the recognition that assimilation endangered their ethnic identity, as scholar William Douglass assessed:

> Persons who clung to their native language and who continued to manifest Old World life-ways were suspect. However, the cumulative effects of two World Wars, the Great Depression and increasingly restrictive U.S. immigration legislation meant that by the 1950s nearly half a century had transpired since America's gates had opened wide to the world's (or at least to Europe's) "huddled masses." As the numbers of new immigrants dwindled and the ethnic neighborhoods aged and withered, it was time for second thoughts. What had we lost in demanding that our forefathers renounce their ethnic essence in order to become Americans?[6]

Several dynamic Boise Basques grappled with what had been lost in the Americanization process. These included Juanita "Jay" Hormaechea, Joe Eiguren, and Jimmy Jausoro, among others. Their stories follow one theory that most second-generation members of an immigrant group question their identity and search for ethnic expression, which some also state is a crisis of self-identification. Some Tartekoak believed that their ethnic expression was imbalanced, as the pendulum had swung toward American assimilation rather than to the retention of their unique ethnicity. Fewer Basques gathered as a separate ethnic group, and interest in Basque cultural traditions waned. These local Boise Basque leaders worked to reverse the loss of Basque culture to Americanization as they emphasized the Basque part of their dual identity, using traditional Basque dance, language, and music.

TARTEKOAK

This first push to resurrect Basque cultural community was in defiance of those who "predicted a gloomy future for the survival of their culture" due to the "children of immigrants [who] were Americanizing and discarding typical Basque cultural traits at a rapid pace."[7] Some believe that it was Juanita "Jay" Hormaechea's 1949 *Boise Music Week* production, "Song of the Basque," that marked a cultural shift. "Song of the Basque" brought notoriety to the Basques of Boise, which sparked welcome interest in the culture from non-Basques. It also resurrected the ancient principle of auzolan among the Tartekoak.

1949 Boise Music Week production, "Song of the Basque." Photo courtesy Basque Museum and Cultural Center, Boise, Idaho.

This successful display of Basque culture provided the impetus for some Tartekoak to push for a new place to connect with their ethnic group, away from the larger American society. This ultimately spurred the creation of a Basque-only organization, *Euzkaldunak*, that began construction of Boise's Basque Center in 1949 and finished it in 1950. The Center would be open only to Basques who could prove their ancestry.

Residences

Tartekoak mostly raised their families in single-family residences among larger non-Basque culture during this time. Private family residences blurred the dual Tartekoak into the homogenous American neighborhood grid. However, the Tartekoak home still represented cultural transmission, and family was the primary transmitter of Basque culture. Internally, Tartekoak continued their Basque cultural traditions and language at home, but externally, they conformed to American social practices.

Tartekoak homes rarely, if ever, displayed ornamentation that would mark it as a Basque residence externally. These homes also did not emulate the distinctive baserri farmhouse style of the Old Country. Although some Basque families moved away from the ethnic boardinghouse enclaves, they retained their close cultural connections with other Basques by clustering as smaller family groups into neighborhoods such as Boise's North End. They may have adopted American ways outwardly, but they still retained their ethnicity within the confines of the home.

LEKUAK: THE BASQUE PLACES OF BOISE, IDAHO

The dual nature of this generation blurred the lines of family roles, and their places. Homes became schools, as Basque children helped their parents and other Amerikanuak navigate the social barriers of language and ethnicity — something that was usually learned at home. For instance, Teresa Aldape tutored her cousin Pancho on school grounds, who had arrived in Boise at the age of fourteen, unable to speak English. Her goal was to help Pancho learn English and American ways so that he could not only be promoted to a classroom with kids his same age and size, but also could learn American customs, or as Teresa once said, "proper things like carrying books for the girls, manners, and how best to talk, walk and dance." [8]

Graduation from an American high school was a priority. Many Amerikanuak parents expected, if not forced, their Tartekoak children to acquire college educations. Julio Bilbao recalled, "There was one thing we understood from the beginning. The message was that education is the most important thing in the world, and if you're going to have opportunities, you've got to have an education. So it was just expected that we were going to go on to school." [9] The Tartekoak, therefore, often left their Basque homes for school in other locations, which began to connect Tartekoak to non-Basques.

Birthday party at the Modern, c. 1931, with some attendees dressed in American military apparel. Photo courtesy Basque Museum and Cultural Center.

Tartekoak completed their American educations, gained employable skills, served in war, and acquired occupations and professional careers in the greater non-Basque society. Tartekoak were distinctively different from their Old Country ancestors and their Amerikanuak parents, because they were the first to make a living with their minds, not their hands. [10] Their places, therefore, were far from the hills and Basque-only enclaves.

TARTEKOAK

Workplaces

Some Tartekoak embraced their hyphenated Basque-American identities that were not so obviously ethnic. The previous Amerikanuak generation's workplaces, whether they were boardinghouses in town or sheepcamps in the hills, were sole places of work where the immigrants also lived. Instead, the Tartekoak often worked away from their living places, marking this generation's shift to independently-operated businesses or jobs in town separate from the home. More than ever before, this generation purchased homes and property, established businesses and worked for non-Basque companies. These were significant achievements for an ethnic group whose parents had only dreamed of land, home, or business ownership.

The emergence of Basques in businesses signaled that the Tartekoak had inched further toward American assimilation. From boxing to barbershops, restaurants to grocery stores, Basques established businesses amid non-Basques. Many of this generation's workplaces were more "mainstream America," with little to no outward expression of their Basque identity. This was a shift from their parents' internal, ethnically segregated places. William Douglass noted that this generation "had learned the hard way to limit expressions of their heritage to the privacy of the home or the semiprivate context of the Basque hotels found in the towns of the sheep-raising districts."[11]

The Americanized business names of Tartekoak that carried very little, if any, evidence of Basque ancestry. Boiseans now patronized Ed Garro's Barber Shop, unaware that Eustaquio Garroguerricaechevarria owned and operated the business.[12] Justo and Angeles Aldape Murelaga named their store the Corner Grocery and A-1 Meats.[13] Brothers José (Joe or "Berritxu") and Benito "Benny" Garate operated their own taxi company, Idan-ha Taxi, out of the Idanha Hotel at 928 Main Street from 1932 to 1945. They eventually operated the Boulevard Service Station, located near the intersection of Grove Street and Capitol Boulevard.[14] These were outwardly American places, not Basque.

Tartekoak businesses maintained close connections to their Basque community despite operating under the banner of American assimilation. Many Basques operated barbershops in town that served non-Basques, although they remained deeply connected to fellow Basques. Basque barbershops were a smaller substitute for the communal gathering places of the Amerikanuak. The Basque barbers and their clientele would speak Euskara to catch up on community news, share sports tales (and bets), and extend support for Basque-owned business. As with some other Basque businesses during this time, Basque barbershop proprietors advertised with more Americanized labels. Interestingly, they retained individual identity by almost always naming the business after the barber, who almost always had assumed an Americanized first name: Ed Garro's Barber Shop, Vicente Echeverria's Vince's Barber Shop, Cecil Sarriarte's Cecil's Barber Shop, and Al Berro's Barber Shop.[15] "Pete" Mendieta, known in Boise as "Barbero," operated his iconic barbershop in the Egyptian Theatre Building for thirty-three years, serving an extensive Basque and non-Basque clientele.[16] Basque barbershops were primarily workplaces, but they also served as Tartekoak social gathering spots. Tartekoak workplaces epitomize the concept of ethnic duality, as can be seen by Basques who used Americanized business names publicly rather than their ethnic surnames or Basque words to label the business.

TARTEKOAK BUSINESSES
Basque Businesses, American Names

1. Vicente "Vince" Echeverria, "Vince's Barbershop." Photo courtesy Vince's Barbershop Facebook page. 2. "Early Boise Taxi Service," José (Joe) "Berritxu" and Benito "Benny" Garate, 1915-1930. Photo courtesy Basque Museum and Cultural Center. 3. Justo and Angeles Aldape Murelaga, "Corner Grocery and A-1 Meats," c. 1944. Photos from Idaho Food Dealer Magazine, 1958, courtesy Murelaga-Aldape famiiles. 4. Pete "Barbero" Mendieta at "O.K. Barber Shop," 1915-1960. Photo courtesy Basque Museum and Cultural Center. 5. "The Shoetorium," John L. Luque, 1937-1977. Photo courtesy Basque Museum and Cultural Center.

TARTEKOAK

Morris Hill Cemetery: St John's Section

Bicandi. Uberuaga. Garmendia. These, and many other Basque surnames, grace the headstones in Boise's Morris Hill Cemetery, mostly in the St. John's Catholic Church sections four through thirteen.[17] Church and city records demonstrate that Basques chose their burial places based upon three reasons: a desire to be buried among the one's family, among the Basque community, and religious preference to be buried in the Catholic section of the cemetery. Church and mortuary records indicate that families almost always contacted their parish priest immediately prior to or upon death for the administration of last rites and sacraments, along with requests for a Catholic funeral.[18] Many Basques purchased family burial plots in the St. Johns' Catholic section at Morris Hill to ensure that generations of relatives could be buried together.

If Basques had no family in America, the task of making end-of-life decisions sometimes rested on boardinghouse proprietors such as Mateo Arregui. Arregui was known to generously cover funeral expenses, which ensured that Basque immigrants could be buried in the St. John's section with fellow Basques.[19] Basque mutual aid societies also set aside special funds to assist with Basque funeral and burial costs, and the Sociedad de Soccoros Mutuos provided funeral insurance for their members.[20]

The Tartekoak generation was the first to bury their parents and fellow foreign-born Basques in public American cemeteries rather than in ancestral burial grounds or local Old Country village cemeteries, called *hilarrieta*. A visit to the St. John's section at Morris Hill Cemetery tells the story of those who chose to build lives in another place far from their homeland.

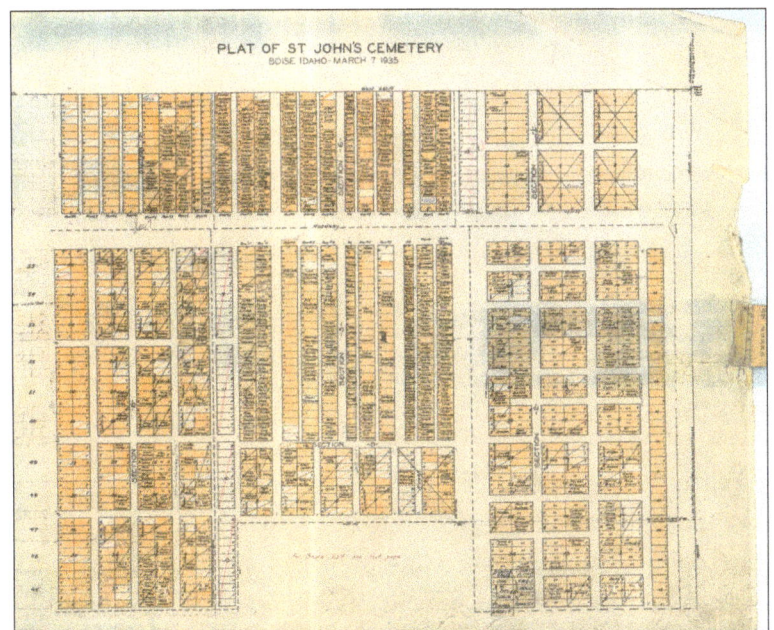

Morris Hill Cemetery, St. John's Section plot map, 1935. Photo courtesy City of Boise, Department of Parks and Recreation.

LEKUAK: THE BASQUE PLACES OF BOISE, IDAHO

Some achieved their dreams and some fell short, but the cemetery demonstrates most Basques lived and died within their ethnic circle. It seems fitting that their final earthly places were shared with one another as a powerful expression of ethnicity and cultural community. The cemetery is a Basque place that honors cultural persistence with visible markers for those left behind to honor and respect their ancestors — and their homeland places.

Temporary Places: Basque Picnics and Mutual Aid Society Events

Although the Tartekoak generation had become a "hyphenated" group that balanced being Basque and being American, their Basque roots were still evident: "they saw their future in America, yet some felt it was important to hold on to elements of the past culture."[21] The need to retain connections with their Basque part of identity prompted Tartekoak to find ways to gather as an ethnic group because the communal boardinghouses were no longer available.

The Tartekoak resorted to group events in outdoor places, or in rented spaces where they could share language, food, and customs with other Basques. They attended summer picnics in local city parks, Barber, Dry Creek, or the Mode Country Club. Some of the mutual aid societies were sources of communal activity, and often those groups hosted charity functions within the Basque community in homes, churches, and social halls.

One social organization during this period was the Basque Girl's Club, formed in 1936. These women held regular meetings at one another's homes and hosted Basque social events, usually with community service goals. Their civic efforts included holiday parties for Basque children, fundraisers, and blankets for war efforts.[22] Tartekoak tried to speak English as much as possible publicly, mindful that Euskara was an undeniable ethnic marker in the greater American realm. Basque Girl's Club member Jay Hormaechea confessed to lapsing into their native language, "We start out in English, then just fall into [Basque]. Habit, I guess. It's easier... We're Americans first, you understand, but we are proud of our Basque heritage too."[23]

Basque picnics were common in the 1940s at local parks. Photos courtesy Basque Museum and Cultural Center, Boise, Idaho.

TARTEKOAK

This women's club was integral to cultural retention, as the women contributed to the inner Basque circle with events and activities, and Euskara was maintained. Their activities were tied to place, although they resorted to temporary places such as halls and rotated private residences. This association, one of several during the Tartekoak such as the mutual aid societies, drew attention to the absence of a central spot for Basque social or recreational activities in Boise.

The Basque Girls' Club began as a knitting group. It grew into a civic organization that helped children, communities, and soldiers during the war. Photo courtesy Basque Museum and Cultural Center, Boise, Idaho.

Basques socialized at clubs and bars, such as Augustin and Francisca "Patxa" Belaustegui's Chico Club, that opened in 1935 as part of their boardinghouse at 117 Grove Street. The Chico Club served Basque meals and drinks for a membership fee of one dollar, and annual dues of an additional dollar.[24] Reflective of Tartekoak dual ethnicity, the Chico Club accepted dues from Basques and non-Basques, and English was spoken as well as Euskara. The Chico Club met the needs of Basque social gatherings, and it also acknowledged the reality of Basques operating in the larger American society.

If dueling identities were not enough to challenge the Tartekoak during this period, internal conflict also arose in the Tartekoak community. John Archabal (formerly Juan Achabal), one of the community's leaders, mediated between two competing Basque mutual aid organizations, La Sociedad de Socorros Mutuos and La Fraternidad Vasca Americana. The two groups were opposed to one another on several issues, and Archabal sought to finally dispel the contention among these two Basque groups in 1929. Archabal devised the Boise Sheepherders' Ball, a charity fundraiser that sought to set aside their differences and join together with common civic cause. Archabal created this annual Christmas dance and lamb auction to raise much-needed funds for Basques in need of fiscal support for medical issues, family misfortune, or other matters of dire need.

LEKUAK: THE BASQUE PLACES OF BOISE, IDAHO

Archabal was extremely successful in his effort to unite the Basques by focusing their energies on others in need.[25] By 1936, the fundraiser grew beyond the inner ethnic group, with non-Basque participation and influences from the greater American society such as contemporary popular music in addition to traditional Basque music for the dance. That year, the *Boise Capitol News* covered Archabal's popular community gathering, "Black-eyed sons and daughters of the Pyrenees danced their beloved 'jota' with snapping fingers and nimble feet Friday evening at the annual Sheepherder's Ball... Basque musicians, playing the Old World tunes, can be heard at one end of the hall [Jimmy Jausoro's famed Basque band] and at the same time an American orchestra is playing at the other end."[26]

The story underscores the Tartekoak generations' dual ethnic expression: they were living partly in the Basque world, and partly in the American. Their dual ethnic expression also led to inner conflict of identity as well as community division. Regardless, Basques united for this annual Christmas event that contributed thousands of dollars to well-deserved recipients of the donations.[27] The Sheepherder's Ball was significant for three reasons. It unified Basques in a communal cause, it addressed the duality of Basque and American identity, and it represented the need for a central, more permanent location for the Basques to gather. Today, the Sheepherders' Ball remains one of Boise's biggest social gatherings and charity fundraisers, for Basques and non-Basques. Likely due to Archabal's vision, the Sheepherder's Ball at the Basque Center is testament to the power of community cohesion, and the influence this event had over the transition from temporary places to permanent ones.

The Annual Sheepherder's Ball, Riverside Dance Hall, 1948. Photos courtesy Basque Museum and Cultural Center, Boise, Idaho.

Basque gatherings in temporary places during the Tartekoak generation were precursors to the larger traditional festivals for which Boise has become internationally renowned. These bursts

TARTEKOAK

of cultural activity in temporary gathering spots rather than in permanent Basque places confirm ethnic identity, but with an important distinction: Tartekoak begin to include non-Basques. This was a cultural shift during the Tartekoak generation. The temporary gathering places reflected the evolution from Basques to Basque-Americans, and with that, the Tartekoak widened the circle beyond the core ethnic group.

Most boardinghouses in the Tartekoak were in decline, so Basques usually ate meals as smaller family units in their residential neighborhoods. This dispersion drove Basques from communal boardinghouse kitchens and tables of the past. The Ysursa family chose to honor the Basques' important ethnic practice of communal food sharing by opening the second floor of their Valencia boardinghouse as a restaurant. When Ysursas placed an advertisement in the newspaper for restaurant's traditional Basque cuisine, it marked a societal transformation of identity.[28] Tartekoak had moved outside their inner circle, by expressing dual Basque and American identity, which influenced the transformation of Basque-only boardinghouse kitchens and eating areas into the public non-Basque places. Restaurants became a mark of the Tartekoak that contributed to cultural persistence, where culture was sustained by also including a broader non-Basque patronage, literally — to the table. Today, Basque restaurants are often the last vestiges of external Basque ethnic expression in communities in the American West.

The Ysursa family's boardinghouse, the Valencia, advertised dining on Idaho Street, 1941-1969, and 1969-1972). Photo courtesy Basque Museum and Cultural Center, Boise, Idaho.

LEKUAK: THE BASQUE PLACES OF BOISE, IDAHO

Boise's Basque Center

As the ethnic circle broadened, some Basques worried that their language and cultural traditions were headed for extinction. Jay Hormaechea feared that Basque culture would be absorbed into the larger American culture. This spurred her to begin traditional Basque dance lessons in 1948, acknowledging that dance and music were foundational to the preservation of the culture into the next generations. She taught Basques of all ages, from little children to adults, in rental halls and temporary places since there were no communal gathering spots to practice. The generational impact of these dance lessons during the close of the Tartekoak generation was significant. Former Hormaechea dance student and founding Oinkari dancer Al Erquiaga said that his parents enrolled he and his sister because they ascribed to the belief that if they did not actively support Basque culture at that time, it could be lost.

Jay's 1949 Boise Music Week production, the "Song of the Basque," drew thousands of attendees to the dress rehearsal and show. Representative of the Tartekoak generation, this seminal cultural event also occurred in a temporary place. It balanced Basque and American culture, as both "God Bless America" and "Gore Amerika" were both sung in the two respective languages.[29] The "Song of the Basque" rekindled pride in being Basque, and it balanced Tartekoak dual identity between ancestral heritage and American community. It spurred interest in the Basques by those outside the culture. It also called attention to the lack of communal space for Basques to again share their common language, food, and customs, including dance. The need for a permanent Basque communal place in Boise was even more clear to the Tartekoak. Place, in other words, had become a driving force for cultural persistence.

In 1949, five hundred charter members founded Euzkaldunak, Inc. with the intent to build a Basque social center.[30] A group of

Juanita "Jay" Hormaechea led the 1949 Boise Music Week production, "Song of the Basque." Photos courtesy Basque Museum and Cultural Center, Boise, Idaho.

TARTEKOAK

Basques sold two hundred thousand dollars worth of bonds to purchase a lot at the corner of Sixth and Grove Streets, near the once-thriving Basque enclave of the Amerikanuak generation. Meaningfully, the lot was adjacent to the Uberuaga boardinghouse, on the spot where Hermenegilda Uberuaga once gardened outside her Basque boardinghouse at 607 Grove Street.[31] Basques gathered in the tradition of auzolan to build the Center with their bare hands: the etxea of the Tartekoak. By 1950 a bar, basement meeting rooms, restrooms, and upstairs card room were ready for use. The second construction phase added a main dance hall, a basement dining area, and a kitchen.[32]

The Basque Center at 601 Grove Street honored the Amerikanuak boardinghouse tradition of communal gathering. A critical difference, however, was that the new Basque Center was not a living space. The social and economic underpinnings of the Tartekoak were completely different from the previous generation. Tartekoak had evolved into a dual ethnic group, and the American part of this reality affected the form and function of their places.

Membership in this sponsoring organization reached into Basque roots, however. Euzkaldunak required proof of Basque heritage or marriage to a person of Basque descent. This is still true today.[33] Boise's Euzkaldunak Basque Club endures as one of the largest Basque organizations in the United States, with 1100 members.[34] Euzkaldunak is responsible for the ownership and operation of the Basque Center that includes space for dance and music practice, weddings, and cultural events. It is open to the public for rentals and the bar, but otherwise only Basques have access to the Center's activities, facilities, and management. Boise's Basque Center was the only place of this generation built by Basques, solely for Basques. The Basque Center was a tribute to the Amerikanuak legacy. In turn, it is also a tribute to the steadfast dedication of the Tartekoak generation to Basque cultural preservation in American society.

Dance practice at the Basque Center. Photo courtesy Basque Museum and Cultural Center, Boise, Idaho.

LEKUAK: THE BASQUE PLACES OF BOISE, IDAHO

Conclusion

Most Tartekoak had moved out of the older immigrant generation's ethnic enclave, and they no longer used boardinghouses for living or social quarters. For the most part, the days of communal living and employment in the hills were relegated to the past. Basque residences and workplaces became integrated into larger society, virtually indistinguishable as ethnic places. The cemetery retained expression of ethnic identity, but only identifiable through Basque symbol or surname. Tartekoak experienced a crisis of ethnic identity due to dual Basque and American forces. They also were divided as a group socially and politically on both American and homeland fronts.

The Tartekoak aligned precisely with Phinney's second stage of ethnic identification crisis, as John Bieter noted: "When asked how they identify themselves, as Basques or Americans, the second generation individuals responded with all possible combinations: Basque, Basque-American, and American-Basque." [35] The lack of Basque-only places during this generation revealed the reality, though, that the Tartekoak's future rested not in the homeland, but in America.

Carmelo Urza's "Modern Period," (beginning in 1948), aligns historically with the period when Boise's Basque leaders were resurrecting their culture with work on the production of "Song of the Basque." Urza contended that assimilation pushed the upward mobility of the Tartekoak, and therefore influenced a positive change in their external social image. This can be seen in the Tartekoak places that represented Basques who had become successful, including single-owner retail businesses.

William Douglass postulated that the American-born children of immigrants rejected the cultural heritage of their parents, and therefore did not express their identity fully. This does not track with Phinney's notion that asserts second-generations were caught in a search for identity during a difficult period of dual ethnic expression. Many also retained some parts of their ethnicity, so they did not reject, they actually chose to exhibit both American and Basque ethnicity. The element of choice becomes more imperative when defining the Egungoak generation, but the Tartekoak laid groundwork for conscious choice of ethnic expression toward the end of the era with "Song of the Basque" and the construction of the Basque Center.

The Tartekoak supported social theories of second-generation identity crisis; assimilation into the greater American melting pot; and the desire to externally express dual Basque and American ethnicity. For instance, the street-facing sign at the Basque Center is in English. No Euskara words appear anywhere externally on the building. The duality of Euzkaldunak's Basque Center is in its very name, and

TARTEKOAK

in its mission to serve two publics: the internal Basque culture and the larger non-Basque community. Membership in Euzkaldunak remains restricted to Basques today. Most events at the Basque Center are for Basques unless the public is contributing fiscal support, such at its public bar or for event rentals. The Basque Center is a place that remains a symbol of Basque cultural persistence today.

Temporary places served an important role in both the Basque community and the retention of ethnic heritage in Boise. These places evolved into external, public efforts in the later Egungoak generation such as Jaialdi, San Inazio, and the Oinkari Basque Dance Club's famed Chorizo Booth. It was this new public acknowledgment of Basqueness that enabled cultural sharing with those outside the circle, which in itself was a step toward enabling cultural persistence. The places of the Tartekoak generation underscored the duality of being Basque *and* American. They foreshadowed what was to come in the 1960s with the Egungoak generations, when "being Basque" became legitimized, and their places became more public and externally-focused as their Basque ethnic identity was achieved.

The Basque Center was built by Basques, for Basques. By 1950, this was a permanent place for social gatherings. Photo courtesy Basque Museum and Cultural Center, Boise, Idaho.

CHAPTER 3 – HIRU
EGUNGOAK

Cyrus Jacobs-Uberuaga boardinghouse. Original photo courtesy Erin Ann Jensen. Digital photo illustration by Meggan Laxalt Mackey.

Liturgical dancing at the altar at The Cathedral of St. John the Evangelist during the annual Basque Festival in Boise, Idaho. Photo courtesy Meggan Laxalt Mackey.

CHAPTER 3 – HIRU ‖ EGUNGOAK
Public Places of Shared Learning (1960s – Present)

What the son wishes to forget, the grandson wishes to remember.
Marcus Lee Hansen, *The Problem of the Third Generation Immigrant*

EGUNGOAK IS TRANSLATED FROM THE EUSKARA WORD *EGUNGO*, MEANING "THOSE OF TODAY," which represents the third generation, the grandchildren of first generation immigrants.[1] Egungoak, who may be of mixed ancestral heritage, often express their ethnicity through conscious choice and inclusivity of non-Basques. Many actively celebrate Basque heritage, both internally and externally. This generation led an energetic charge to display their ethnicity publicly, and they embrace cultural plurality. A fundamental part of the Egungoak psyche is education. To fully comprehend the influence of education on the Egungoak generation, a short history of the development of Basque educational institutions, including some efforts outside of Boise are discussed.

Egungoak Basques share their culture on the Basque Block during the San Inazio Basque Festival in Boise, Idaho. Photos courtesy Gay Thornton Boonen.

LEKUAK: THE BASQUE PLACES OF BOISE, IDAHO

Cultural Purality on Display

Egungoak generation members were products of the "cultural identity pride" movement of the 1960s and 1970s, when a groundswell of renewed pride in ethnic heritage occurred for many Americans, regardless of generation or ethnic identification.[2] This pushed Egungoak to connect with others of their Basque heritage in the Basque Country, other American cities, and even other diaspora locations globally. Due to transportation and technology, seemingly once-disparate Basque places suddenly were connected, which resulted in a global effort to recapture Basque. This phenomenon also occurred with other ethnic groups in America, spurring searches for family histories, the creation of ethnic dance troupes, classes in multicultural studies, and travel to homeland countries. It was in many ways, a unifying movement for the generation that had experienced great social divide in America over the Vietnam War, racial issues, and other public issues.

Historian Jill Gill likened this occurrence to the previous generation, "Just as World War II had encouraged unity under 'Americanization,' so too did the cultural pride movement.[3] This movement propelled Egungoak Basques to learn more about the cultural heritage of their grandparents, which placed the value of education at the forefront of their efforts. Some Egungoak places that have an educational focus include the Basque Museum and Cultural Center and its Cyrus Jacobs-Uberuaga boardinghouse, the Unmarked Basque Graves Projects, Boise State University's Basque Studies Program, and the Boiseko Ikastola.

If the Amerikanuak were characterized by being a singular, internal Basque culture, and the Tartekoak modeled duality of Basque and American culture, the Egungoak represented a new era of external cultural plurality. Egungoak were proudly Basque even if their ancestry had become diluted. They chose to acknowledge their Basque roots, and sometimes gave them priority over other parts of their ancestry. Basques were joined by non-Basques who spoke Euskara, danced the *jota*, sang in the *Biotzetik Choir*, and played the *txistu* to help revive and preserve Basque culture.

Mixed cultural identity was gaining social acceptance in the United States in the 60s and 70s, especially with increased social, educational, and economic mobility. Many Egungoak intermarried, and a number of them married spouses of non-Basque descent.

Public display of cultural plurality was a hallmark of the. Egungoak Photo courtesy Meggan Laxalt Mackey.

Multiculturalism aligned with the greater American story of the same period, when the country had been preoccupied with the Vietnam War, civil rights, and racial tension. Alex Haley's book *Roots* encouraged personal quests for knowledge about family histories, and public awareness was focused on the plurality of America's various ethnic and racial groups.

William Douglass noted the impact of multiculturalism on the greater American culture, "A renewal of ethnic pride was ... critical ... a pride that could only be ratified through a new understanding of each group's worth and past contributions to American culture."[4]

EGUNGOAK PLACES

Egungoak experienced greater educational and employment opportunity than the Tartekoak generation, which encouraged more social, economic, and geographic mobility. This resulted in very different Basque places: they were more public and culturally diverse than ever before, frequently away from the "familiar relatives and neighborhoods of one's childhood."[5]

The physical separation from one's family and core ethnic group encouraged integration with larger American society. Few Egungoak had traveled to the Basque Country though, and even fewer spoke Euskara, since they had been raised by Tartekoak parents who usually self-identified as "American," or at least "Basque-American." Many Egungoak, therefore, had to look outside the home and beyond their American community to reconnect with their Basque culture. Egungoak engaged in an external quest for information and connection to their heritage. Once they gained the knowledge, they shared it with others, often publicly.

EGUNGOAK
Public Places of Shared Learning (1960s - Present)

- **Cultural Plurality on Display**
- **The Influence of Education**
  - **Basque Museum and Cultural Center**
  - **Anduiza Fronton**
  - **Basque Center Façade**
- **Unmarked Graves Projects**
  - **Boiseko Ikastola**
  - **The Basque Mural**

LEKUAK: THE BASQUE PLACES OF BOISE, IDAHO

The Influence of Education

Immigrant Amerikanuak grandparents had established education as a primary goal for their children. The Tartekoak acquired that education, which provided opportunities that their parents had never realized. Education was a primary influence in the Egungoak generation, and they embraced it to extend their cultural knowledge, supporting a reconnection with their Basque heritage. Some Egungoak chose to learn more about Basque history, culture, and language through university courses, private lessons, independent research, and international travel. The Egungoak's grandparents had chosen to migrate out of the Basque Country, and a good number of Egungoak made a conscious choice to return.

The Egungoak, descendants of Basque immigrants, led an ethnic revival using educational tools to move it along. They worked hard to reestablish cultural identity by learning to speak Euskara, practicing ancient dance and music, and improving their knowledge of Basque history and politics. The Egungoak also instituted the blurring of geographic boundaries, sharing education among Basques outside their cities and states. Improved automobiles, air travel, and technology greatly aided the transformation of ethnic identity, where the sphere of influence broadened beyond one's local community. For instance, Boise Basques worked with Nevada Basques on scholarly endeavors, and the Chino, California dancers performed with dancers from Buffalo, Wyoming. *North American Basque Organizations* (NABO) was formed in 1973, and Basques from diaspora nations collaborated globally with each other and the Euro-Basques in the Basque Country.[6] This also ushered in greater collaboration with Basques in the diaspora and homeland, with study abroad opportunities, international projects, shared academic research, collaborative business and trade, athletics, and relationships with the Basque Autonomous Government.

The Basque Government and American Basque entities dedicated fiscal and political support of educational efforts, which resulted in increased communication, commerce, politics, and partnership-based shared culture. The Egungoak story therefore moved beyond the local, and connected U.S. Basques to Euro-Basques, other diaspora Basques, and those outside the ethnic group who were simply interested in Basque culture. People and place truly intersect in this generation, aided by education and shared communication.

Basque collaboration in the Egungoak era.

EGUNGOAK

Egungoak places also indicate the importance of time: this generation experienced rapid social change from the 1960s until today, not just in America, but globally. Egungoak places were the result of the evolution from small ethnic enclaves to broader American neighborhoods to the global community. Many Egungoak actively shared their rediscovered roots with pride, inclusively, in public places.

In 1959, a bold move to publicly share Basque culture on a large scale in the U.S. was the first-ever Basque Festival in Sparks, Nevada (part of the Reno-Sparks metropolitan area). This festival was organized in large part by Tartekoak Basques who were operating under a transition to the Egungoak era. Reno and Boise Basques worked together to host the festival at Richard L. "Dick" Graves *Nugget Casino* in Sparks, led by Committee members Dick Graves, John Ascuaga, Pete Echeverria, Pete Supera, Dominic Gascue, Martin Esain, Joe Micheo, Paul Parraguirre, and brothers Robert and John Laxalt.[7]

This event was the catalyst for the current Basque festival cycle that occurs throughout the American West today. Communities small and large modeled their Basque festivals after the transformative Nevada event, sharing food, dance, music, and other aspects of Basque culture with a largely non-Basque population. Most of these festivals are held through the summer, akin to those held in the Basque Country around traditional agricultural activities such as planting and harvest, the solstice, and and patron saint feast days. Boise Egungoak Basques transformed small, internal, localized efforts into their widely recognized external celebration, *Jaialdi*, an international event that occurs every five years and hosts thousands of visitors in the capital city.[8]

Precursors to large Basque festivals included the first Basque Festival in Sparks, Nevada, in 1959. Photo courtesy University of Nevada, Reno, Center for Basque Studies.

LEKUAK: THE BASQUE PLACES OF BOISE, IDAHO

In 1960, Boise's acclaimed *Oinkari Basque Dancers* began to perform, barely on the heels of the inaugural Nevada Basque Festival. Initially, the group performed within a short radius of Boise in the Basque Center, on the streets, and for public events. This dance group later performed at the Seattle World's Fair in 1962. By 1964 they stunned crowds at the World's Fair in New York.[9] Although some point to Jay Hormaechea's "Song of the Basque" as the seminal event that rejuvenated Basque pride, the Oinkari Dancers' efforts of 1960s exposed Basque culture externally, well beyond Boise. The Basque Block is one spot in Boise where there Oinkaris dance today, but they also perform liturgical dances at St. John's Cathedral, and traditional dances in a host of public places in the U.S. and abroad. Public places are essential to the transmission of ethnic culture by educating, and even including, others in cultural activity.

Boise Oinkari Dancers performing at the New York World's Fair in 1964. Photo courtesy University of Nevada, Reno, Center for Basque Studies.

The Basques call themselves *Eukzaldunak*, which literally means "those who speak Basque."[10] This self-identification is the hallmark of Basque identity, anywhere in the world. Members of the Egungoak generation have engaged in a serious effort to recover Euskara by speaking the language, and some also have immersed themselves in historical and cultural studies, which they view as key to cultural preservation. Because of this, a significant change occurred: Basques studies became institutionalized. Carmelo Urza supported this assertion with his Basque institutional phases, and some of Boise's Basque places reflect educational institutions as another critical element of Basque persistence today.

Egungoak educational efforts took a serious first step in 1972 when Congress appropriated funds for the national Ethnic Heritage Studies Program Act. This paved the way for a $52,285 grant through the National Endowment for the Humanities to establish a Basque Studies Program in Boise.[11] The goals were to create a robust program with Basque language and cultural studies, a Basque library, and a six-week summer study abroad program to the Basque Country. Comparatively, in 2017 dollars, the grant would have been worth $293,599. Boise's Basque Studies Program sponsored language classes, cultural studies, a Basque choir, music and dance, and the 1972 Holiday Basque Festival, the precursor to Boise's Jaialdi.[12] Boise's Basque Studies Program was a substantial effort, spurred on by Egungoak Basques to apply education to the cultural revival, with the goal of cultural persistence into the future.

Place was a central factor in the next phase of the program when in 1974, Boise State University's Pat Bieter, his wife Eloise, and others established the first study abroad program in the Basque Country in the Gipuzkoan town of Oñati. Pat Bieter recognized that in order for the program to be successful, the students needed immersion in Basque language and culture. That connection could not occur without physically locating the students in the Basque Country. That fall, seventy-five students, five faculty members, and the entire seven-person Bieter family became the first American academics to live and study on Basque soil.[13] One Egungoak student of the Boise-Oñati program insightfully remarked, "To know who you are and where you come from is important in directing where you're going in the future."[14]

This underscored Phinney's third and final stage of ethnic identity development: *ethnic identity achievement*, which underscored the third generation's security in their identity and clarity of purpose in regaining their ethnic heritage.[15] The language-intensive Oñati study abroad program continued until 1980 when Boise State University, University of Nevada, Reno, and other schools formed a larger consortium program in Donostia-San Sebastián.[16]

The seeds of Boise's Basque educational places were planted during this seminal study abroad program that bridged the Basque Country and America. Numerous collaborative educational efforts throughout the Egungoak's period firmly established educational places as a critical factor of cultural persistence. These places support Basque culture and are some of the primary places that ensure its preservation. To name a few,

The Boise-Oñati Study Abroad Program (1974-1975) led by Dr. Pat Bieter, was a seminal educational effort for Egungoak in the United States and the Basque Country. Photo courtesy Boise State University, Basque Studies Program.

LEKUAK: THE BASQUE PLACES OF BOISE, IDAHO

Boise's Basque Museum and Cultural Center, Boiseko Ikastola, Boise State University, and the Cenarrusa Foundation for Basque Culture, as well as the University of Nevada, Reno's William A. Douglass Center for Basque Studies. Combined, the two universities in Boise and Reno offer courses, student and faculty exchanges, workshops, libraries, and archives for the study of Basques. These institutions support the multi-partner University Studies Abroad Consortium (USAC), with language-based learning in Euskal Herria and other foreign countries.[17] The Etxepare Basque Institute establishes academic chair positions in key diaspora locations. Boise joined Reno as a chair location in 2015 when Etxepare and Boise State University's Basque Studies Program established a new chair in honor of Boise Basque Eloise Garmendia Bieter. It was the first chair position named after a woman. The Egungoak generation's educational places are essential pillars of support to cultural preservation. Carmelo Urza's contention that this period was characterized by the creation of institutions, particularly educational institutions, is quite true.[18]

Basque Museum and Cultural Center

The American-born daughter of a Basque immigrant was almost singlehandedly responsible for establishing one of the most important Basque communal places in the United States: the Basque Museum and Cultural Center. Adelia Garro Simplot was the daughter of Ed Garro, whose barbershop business was a model of Basque community. Adelia used her Basque family's well-earned reputation to focus on cultural pride and preservation in the city of Boise. In the 1980s, Adelia was determined to save an old boardinghouse that was in need of restoration at 607 Grove Street. It was one of the last testaments to the first Basque generation's humble beginnings in Boise. This historic brick home was built by Boise pioneer Cyrus Jacobs in 1864, and it had already been entered into the National Register of Historic Places in 1976. Adelia wanted to preserve this early Boise place that also was a symbol of Basque culture. On November 28, 1983, she purchased the building from José and Hermengilda Uberuaga's children, Serafina Uberuaga Mendiguren, Joe Uberuaga, and Julia Uberuaga Coleman for $60,000 dollars.[19]

EGUNGOAK

Adelia was visionary, but she was not naïve: if Basque culture was to be preserved in Boise by first saving the boardinghouse, it would require a deep fiscal and emotional commitment from local Basques and other citizens, as a whole community. It would require the Old World principle of auzolan — from everyone.

Later in 1985, Adelia led the effort to form the non-profit Basque Cultural Center of Idaho, dedicated to the preservation of Basque history and culture.[20] She established this Cultural Center in the old boardinghouse at 607 Grove, a place immigrant Basques had called home for many years. The articles of incorporation stated that the educational purposes were to "stimulate the interest of the public... in the development and offering of Basque literature and language studies, history, and the assembling and maintenance of a collection of Basque-related artifacts."[21]

Adelia Garro Simplot and her then-husband Richard had been personally paying the mortgage on the property since 1983, and committed to continuing that through December 1986. They deeded it as a gift to the museum organization, "For and in consideration of our love and affection for the Basque heritage and history in the State of Idaho."[22] It was an act that would prove to be in the best cultural and historical interest of the Basques, the City of Boise, and the State of Idaho.

The Basque Museum and Cultural Center, the first museum in America dedicated to Basque heritage, was opened in 1985 with the help of the Basque community and other interested patrons and volunteers. On October 5, 1986, over a thousand people stood on Boise's Grove

The Basque Museum and Cultural Center was first established in the Cyrus Jacobs-Uberuaga boardinghouse at 607 Grove Street by Adelia Garro Simplot. Photo of boardinghouse courtesy Peter Oberlindacher. Photo of Adelia Garro Simplot courtesy Basque Museum and Cultural Center, Boise, Idaho.

Street to attend the museum's inaugural Open House. The Basque Museum and Cultural Center's official dedication occurred June 19, 1987, with support from attendees from Boise to the Basque Country.[23] This was a moment of international pride for Basques of all generations from both the Basque Country and America. It marked the Egungoak's first educational place that was open and inclusive: anyone could enter and learn about Basque history and culture there.

Adelia did not stop with the Museum project to preserve Basque culture. On December 1, 1988, she purchased the 611 Grove Street building adjacent to the boardinghouse for $125,000. This property became the museum exhibit and operations headquarters. Adelia's action was instrumental in preventing the demise of yet another historic Basque building in Boise because property owner Robert F. Barney was ready to demolish the building for another city parking lot.[24] The Basque community coalesced over the museum's extensive list of needs: planning, construction and renovation, flooring, exhibit building, artifact and collection building, painting, administration, a library, and a myriad of other needs for a bona fide cultural museum.

In 2003, the museum embarked on an extensive historic preservation project to restore the boardinghouse at 607 Grove Street to period authenticity so it could be used as a living history museum for public tours. Executive Director Patty Miller and Museum Curator Jeff Johns directed the truly auzolan effort. Basques and non-Basques preserve one of Boise's last-standing symbols of Basque culture. The museum's restoration project added a living dimension to Basque education, and established the project as yet another first for Boise and the American West. The renovated Cyrus Jacobs-Uberuaga boardinghouse was a nod to the past, and a leap to the future. It became a public ethnic symbol of Basque cultural persistence, located in the middle of Boise's Basque Block, a central downtown district.

The Cyrus Jacobs-Uberuaga boardinghouse is restored to both the early Boise period (1864) and the later Amerikanuak period. Photo of boardinghouse dining area courtesy Erin Ann Jensen.

The Basque Museum and Cultural Center has remained a guiding force of cultural maintenance throughout the Egungoak period. Institutionalization of culture through educational places was one way to ensure the Museum's mission "to preserve, promote, and perpetuate Basque history and culture."[25] Another hallmark of the Egungoak period was the effort to maintain this ethnic culture by actively choosing to perform acts that would perpetuate Basque culture, which was also articulated in the museum's mission statement. To achieve this, Egungoak established a physical spot centrally located in town that would not only be accessible to the Basque community, but also to non-Basques who may be interested in learning more about their unique culture. The Basque Museum notes, "As a cultural center, it is a gathering place for events and educational opportunities — in which people of all backgrounds can participate in Basque activities."[26] The museum looked beyond its internal Basque structure, and moved externally by opening its membership and doors to *all* visitors. Anyone, regardless of Basque ancestry, can obtain a membership in this educational organization. It appears to be working, with 862 museum members, 17,787 services on and off-site annually, and over 3,000 schoolchildren are reached by educational programs and activities for over 114 schools.[27]

The Basque Museum and Cultural Center is reflective of Phinney's third phase of ethnic identity achievement, and it has produced steadily increasing interest and support of Basque culture. In contrast, the Basque Center represented a different need. It was established as a social center solely for Basque immigrants and their families, which retained a more internally focused purpose. In order to prevent the decline of ethnicity that Gans and Alba predicted, both approaches may help Boise's Basque places remain as symbols of cultural persistence.

The collective actions of the Egungoak, including educational efforts at the Basque Museum and Cultural Center, have allowed generations of Basques and thousands of others to learn about and celebrate this ethnic group. The Basque Museum and Cultural Center is the quintessential place of public Basque education in the American West — right in the middle of a bustling modern city. The Egungoak generation can be credited with using a sense of place to revitalize Basque culture, using education as a primary link to cultural persistence.

The Basque Museum and Cultural Center, 611 Grove St. Photo courtesy Meggan Laxalt Mackey.

LEKUAK: THE BASQUE PLACES OF BOISE, IDAHO

The Anduiza Fronton: Reclaimed

In 1971 the Idaho Basque Studies Program secured funding for a program "about Basques, but it is a program for all people, Basque and non-Basque," with broadened objectives beyond Basque-only culture, "strengthening cultural pride and preserving cultural characteristics which lend variety and richness to our diverse American society."[28] As part of the Basque Studies Program in 1972, Egungoak Basques entered into an agreement with Briggs Engineering to return the Anduzia Fronton at 619 Grove Street to its original purpose as a Basque handball court. Immediately after the agreement was signed, volunteers cleaned up the fronton space that had served as a storage area for thirty years. The group reroofed the failing structure, installed lights and safety screens, and painted the fronton so that the first pelota classes, player practices, and matches could begin.[29]

To some, this was in defiance of a sociologist who once predicted that the handball courts would "probably remain as ruins when the last foreign-born pelota player has passed away."[30] The Bieter brothers, of the Egungoak generation, noted the cultural gains of the successful reclamation of the American Anduiza Fronton instead, "Refuting earlier predictions about these courts, a group of volunteers painted the court's lines and repaired the roof, and the studies program organized regular pala and handball tournaments."[31]

The Egungoak dream to reclaim the distinctive indoor court was fulfilled when the first public pala/pelota tournament was played in 1976, sponsored by Idaho'ko Euzko Zaleak and Anaiak Danok.[32] Interest swelled in both watching the games and competing in the sport. The fronton, the only distinctively Basque structure that had been transplanted from

A glass window on the Anduiza Fronton door reflects natural light from the tall ceiling. Boiseko Fronton Association members play year-round. Photos courtesy Meggan Laxalt Mackey.

EGUNGOAK

the Old Country to America was back in play, literally. Boise Basques formed the Boise Fronton Association in 1989, with twenty members.[33]

The story did not close there, however. Adelia Garro Simplot, still zealous in her quest to preserve Basque heritage, joined forces with another Boise Basque, Rich Hormaechea. They purchased the historic 1914 Anduiza boardinghouse and fronton from the Briggs family for $255,000 in 1993.[34] They leased the handball court to the Boise Fronton Association, and as with most all Egungoak efforts, anyone is welcome to play for a small membership fee — Basque or not.[35]

Today, pala players use the facility year-round, and women also play the Basque games baleen and goma in the fronton. International and national championships are played there, rivaling play at the only other indoor public court in the United States, in San Francisco, California.

The Anduiza Fronton stands again as a distinctive ethnic place for Basques of all generations, with larger numbers of players and crowds than ever before. This would not have been possible without the hard work — and conscious choice — of Egungoak to claim their ethnic heritage and bring it into the public spotlight. The renovation and purchase of the Anduiza Fronton represents the sports tradition of the Basques. It pays tribute to a time when frontons were integral to the communal aspect of the Basque Country village, as well as the Amerikanuak boardinghouse. Egungoak celebrated the Anduiza Fronton's 100 years in 2014, another testament to place contributing to Basque cultural persistence today.

Players actively practice and compete at the Anduiza Fronton in Boise. Photos courtesy John Bieter and Basque Museum and Cultural Center, Boise, Idaho.

LEKUAK: THE BASQUE PLACES OF BOISE, IDAHO

The Basque Center Façade

In 1972, Egungoak added a distinctive Basque feature to the Basque Center's stark exterior walls that faced both Grove and Sixth Streets: a *baserri* (Basque farmhouse) façade.[36] The previous ordinary, utilitarian concrete building reflected the insular, more inward focus of the previous generations. The Center's simple exterior did little to outwardly express Basque identity.

No places in Boise displayed features that resembled Old World Basque architecture, except for possibly a few stucco residences with red-tiled roofs in Boise's North End, such as the Uranga home on Bannock Street, or homes near the Tartekoak enclave near Fort and 8th Streets. To openly identify with their ethnic heritage, Egungoak members embarked on an ambitious upgrade to the Basque Center's exterior, adding white stucco, wood beams, a red tile roof, iron grates, and double barn-type doors with two large carved wood plaques.

This addition signified a public expression of Basque culture through a visible connection to homeland baserriak. The *ikurriña*, or Basque flag, was eventually added to the American flag. The flying of this flag instilled a deep sense of Basque pride to some members of the Amerikanuak generation, because ikurriñak had been prohibited during the Franco years from 1939 to 1975, under severe penalty and even death; some Basques had been reticent to even raise it publicly in the U.S. during the Amerikanuak and Tartekoak generations, far from Franco's oppression.[37]

The updated Basque Center façade is another example of the Egungoak generation's conscious choice to outwardly express being Basque within the larger American culture. The Basque Center facelift added cultural significance to the older Tartekoak period building because it is one of the few architectural features in Boise that symbolize Basque cultural persistence.

"Zazpiak Bat" is Basque for "The Seven are One." This plaque is on one of two entry doors to the Basque Center. Photo courtesy Meggan Laxalt Mackey.

74

EGUNGOAK

The Unmarked Basque Graves Projects (1997-2017)

In 1993 the Basque Attorney General, Iñaki Goikoetxeta, traveled to Boise for business. He was aware that his grandfather, José Goikoetxeta, who was born in 1890, immigrated to Idaho from Bizkaia to work as a sheepherder. He died in Boise in 1938, leaving a widow and several small children in the homeland. Iñaki searched for his grandfather's grave at Boise's Morris Hill Cemetery, but no one could find the gravesite. This led to the discovery that a number of Basque gravesites in the St. John's Section of Morris Hill Cemetery were unmarked.[38]

Upon making this discovery a Boise Basque, Dolores Totorica, worked to match death records with burial sites at the cemetery. Liz (Arregui-Dick) Hardesty then formed a new effort to continue Dolores's work. She spearheaded a community history research project in 1997 to research more information, especially from funeral home records. Liz was unwavering in her goal to properly honor these Basques in their final resting places. She had a personal stake in this effort as the granddaughter of a long-time Boise boardinghouse operator Mateo Arregui. Liz knew that her *aitona* (grandfather) Mateo, and his first wife Adriana, as well his second wife Maria Dominga Goicoechea, took their role as "second parents" to many of their boarders seriously. Acting as pseudo-parents to many boarders who worked in isolation as herders meant that boardinghouse proprietors assumed many costs for Basques who had no family or funds in the United States. Boardinghouse owners often covered funeral and burial costs. They also conducted the legal business of death, calling authorities, preparing bodies for burial, speaking with priests and arranging funerals, and completing legal paperwork.[39] The boardinghouse operator was sometimes the herder's only friend: in life, and in death.

"You Are Not Forgotten." The Morris Hill Cemetery in Boise honors the memory of Basques who passed away in the United States, far from their homelands. Photos courtesy Robert Kibler.

LEKUAK: THE BASQUE PLACES OF BOISE, IDAHO

Mateo Arregui's signature appears on various documents of deceased boarders who had been at his boardinghouse, such as funeral home records. These clearly note the expenses Arregui covered to ensure decent burials. At times, he worked with Boise's mutual aid societies to help fund additional funeral and burial expenses for these immigrants. The two primary organizations were the La Sociedad de Soccoros Mutuos, founded in 1908 with about two hundred Basque members, and the La Fraternidad Vasca Americana, founded for men in 1928, later conjoined with its women's auxiliary in 1930.

Liz believed that just as her aitona, Mateo, cared for Basque people in life, she too would carry out his legacy by caring for Basques in their afterlife by ensuring they were properly honored.[40] Three years and thousands of volunteer hours later, 130 unmarked Basque graves were discovered. Due to Liz Hardesty's hard work and the volunteers she championed, the research team identified sixty-four "lost" names and located more than sixty graves, giving respect and name recognition to members of the Basque community who were laid to rest at the Morris Hill Cemetery. Liz recorded as much information as possible, painstakingly handwriting minute details about occupation, Basque Country origins, circumstances of death, and burial costs.

When Liz and her team completed the research, they needed to mark the gravesites. Dorothy Bicandi Aldecoa, another Boise Basque woman, generously paid for all of the grave markers of those who were buried there. She also funded a large communal monument in the Basque section at the cemetery to honor Basques whose gravesites could not be located. Today, visitors to the cemetery can see this tall granite stone, adorned with the Basque lauburu symbol and the inscription: "With respect and pride, we honor the memories of our Basque ancestors in this sacred place. You are not forgotten…"[41]

The Hardesty Unmarked Graves Project was completed, but in 2015 at Boise's Jaialdi celebration, Lehendakari Iñigo Urkulla (President of the Autonomous Basque Community), committed to more work on this effort. That next year, the Basque Government initiated another attempt to honor these Basques. They funded a new research project to compile as many records as possible, focusing on the birthplaces of those who were buried at Morris Hill in Boise.

Memorial stone in honor of those whose gravesites could not be located. Photo courtesy Robert Kibler.

EGUNGOAK

Boise State University's Basque Global Collaborative led this next phase, *Artzainak Gogoan*, under the direction of Dr. John Ysursa and project leader Meggan Laxalt Mackey.[42] At first, sheepherder immigrants were focused on, but with the help of the Basque Museum and Cultural Center, the new research revealed that not all those in the Unmarked Graves Project were herders, and few birthplaces were noted in funeral home or cemetery burial records.

Ysursa and Laxalt also led the third and final phases of the Unmarked Graves Projects, *Ahaztu Barik: Remembering our Basque Ancestors*. *Ahaztu Barik* focused on additional data about those with verifiable burial plots, beyond just searching for birthplaces. Working with volunteers Celeste Landa, Dave Lachiondo, Connie Urresti, and museum staff, the team viewed innumerable historic records, including ship manifests and immigration records, city ledgers, death certificates, census data, and church, prison and military records. The research documented a few Basque Country birthplaces, some parent names, death dates, causes of death in America, and plot locations. Researchers also found new grave markers that had been installed by reconnected family members, and several immigrants from other countries such as Italy and Mexico who had previously been identified as Basque in error. Each gravesite was mapped with GPS locations and documented with a photo of the gravesite marker. Lastly, a searchable website was built to enable global access to the more extensive information, ultimately serving the goal of encouraging exchanges among Basques across miles and years. (See http://basquemuseum.eus/research/ahaztu-barik-cemetery-project to learn more.)

The Ahaztu Barik cemetery project used the Basque symbol of the eguzkilore, a dried sunflower, to honor Basques who have passed on.

Ahaztu Barik honored those Basques who were buried in America, ensuring that their lives and memories would never be forgotten. *Ahaztu Barik* used the symbol of the Basque *eguzkilore*, a dried sunflower. Ancient Basques placed eguzkilore over home doorways as the first greeting to anyone who entered a Basque home. It was placed to ward off evil, provide strength, and protect families.

Boise's San Inazio Basque Festival was inaugurated on July 28, 2017, with a ceremony at the Morris Hill Cemetery. Hand-forged metal eguzkilore were placed on fifty-nine gravesites at Morris Hill that had been researched and verified, to symbolize welcome and protection. Gorka Aramburu, director of the

Basque Autonomous Government's Communities Abroad Department, was the keynote speaker. Boise Mayor David Bieter, Aita (Father) Antton Egiguren, the Basque Catholic community's priest from Cathedral of St. John, Dr. John Ysursa, Basque Museum Executive Director Annie Gavica, and members of the *Ahaztu Barik* team spoke. Attendees who attended the ceremony also heard traditional Basque music from Boise's Biotzetik Basque Choir.

Ahaztu Barik was a true *auzolan* endeavor, with many persons from Basque communities abroad and in Boise working together. The effort was instrumental in bringing forward new information about many Basques who were buried at Morris Hill, and provided a new means for public to access that information. These efforts acknowledged that cemetery headstones are permanent markers of one's life, which only tell a portion of one's life story.

The Unmarked Graves Projects remind us that cemeteries are powerful places of ancestry. They also remind us of the circle of life, from generation to generation: *Izan zirelako gara; garelako izango dira*: "because of them we are, and because of us, they will be."

The Ahaztu Barik celebration at Morris Hill Cemetery launched Boise's 2017 San Inazio Basque Festival. Photos courtesy Dennis Mackey.

EGUNGOAK

Boiseko Ikastola

Basque cultural persistence into the future now rests on the shoulders of the *Etorkizunekoak* generation, and the young students of the Boiseko Ikastola will have to lead the way. The Ikastola is the only Basque language preschool outside the Basque Country. It was established as a language immersion preschool in 1988 as a link between the past, present, and future.

During the Franco years (1937-1975), Basques in Euskal Herria operated clandestine schools in nursing homes, churches, garages, and home basements. Brave teachers and parents supported the forbidden ikastola schools, so that Basque children would learn and maintain their native language, Euskara.[43] Dedicated Basques risked this education for their children, even if it could result in political problems, because they recognized the possibility the language could be permanently removed from the Basque people, which was their primary means of identity.[44] The immersion method used to teach language to children was a strong attempt by the Basques to ensure that Euskara did not die out.[45] Years later the Egungoak in America embarked on the same process to recover the language, although this time with open expression of ethnic identity, designed to consciously choose cultural persistence.[46]

In 1998, a group of Boise Basque parents, led by Nerea Lete and her husband Chris Bieter, wanted to ensure that Basque children learned both the language and culture of the Euzkaldunak ("speakers of Basque").[47] They organized the Boiseko Ikastola under the Basque Museum and Cultural Center, gained State Board of Education approval, and reached out to members of the Basque community. Together, auzolan produced the preschool through fiscal, in-kind, and equipment contributions. Many Ikastola teachers are native Euskara speakers who travel to Boise from the Basque Country for several months at a time experience teaching in American schools. Boiseko Ikastola has earned an honorable distinction in both the U.S. and Euskal Herria as the only Basque preschool outside the Basque Country.[48]

Boiseko Ikastola is operated by the Basque Museum and Cultural Center. Photo courtesy Meggan Laxalt Mackey.

LEKUAK: THE BASQUE PLACES OF BOISE, IDAHO

Jeanne Alzola once commented about the first generation's reaction to the establishment of an Ikastola on American soil, if they had been able to witness it, "If they could just see us now! You know our parents and grandparents came here to escape political and economic problems. Many were not allowed to speak Basque. Well look at this! This is a memorial to them."[49] If future generations retain the Basque language, their connections to Basque culture will remain, which will help ensure cultural persistence into the future.

According to co-founder Nerea Lete, the Egungoak "wanted to help our children to learn Euskara and [become] immersed in the Basque culture so they could connect in a very special way with grandparents and Basque-speaking family members here and in the Basque Country."[50] More importantly, the Boise Ikastola is a distinct Basque place. It was intended to lay the groundwork for American-Basques of the future, already of mixed ancestry, to connect Basque culture between time, place, and the generations. Lete noted that the Ikastola serves as "the habia (nest) of Basque culture in Boise. Our children learn about the language and the culture ... the Ikastola helps our youngest generation and young families make an emotional and cultural connection with our elders."[51] The Ikastola is now housed at 1955 Broadway Avenue, in a permanent building owned and operated by the Basque Museum, reflecting a long-term commitment to cultural education.[52]

The Basque Government also plays a major role in this and other educational places in Boise, signaling that connections between the Basque Country and the United States are critical elements of Basque cultural persistence in the U.S. and abroad. Boise Egungoak have maintained strong partnerships among Basques in both countries for many years, which supports the argument that ethnicity is not in decline, but rather, Basque culture is in a state of strong cultural persistence today.

The Boiseko Ikastola may possibly be the most important Basque place yet, as it is dedicated solely to the transmission and maintenance of Basque culture into the future. The youngest generations are learning that ethnicity is shared and global, and that cultural diversity is valued in America today. The Ikastola is a link to the future between the Basques and a broader, more inclusive community, as demonstrated by its open enrollment: non-Basque children are welcomed.

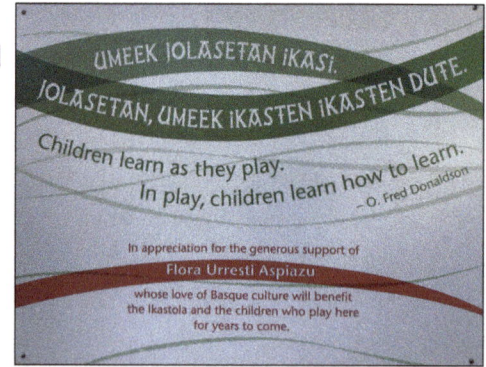

EGUNGOAK

The Basque Mural

A 48-foot-long mural hangs along the backside of the Anduiza Fronton, facing Boise's Capitol Boulevard. This art is the creation of longtime Boise sign artist Noel Weber and an international group of sign painters called the Letterheads. Bill Hueg, the Letterheads leader and renowned muralist, led the project in 2000. To gather more information about the Basques, Hueg accompanied Jose Luis Arrieta, the foreman of the Highland Sheep Company in a sheepcamp, and gained key information from Boise Basques. This collaboration was one of three murals the group painted as part of the Letterheads' 25th annual conference. Yanke's Machine Shop donated the mural panels. The Boise City Department of Arts and History has had this downtown mural cataloged in their Public Arts Collection since its installation. A fund drive is active currently to restore the mural, led by the Basque Museum, Boise City Department of Arts and History, and Boise's Basque Club, Euzkaldunak.[53]

This public art piece draws the observer into a panoramic mural that traces the Basques' journey from Euskal Herria to Boise, Idaho. The colorful piece focuses on *place* as its central theme, highlighting the journey from Old World Basque places to New World places in the American West. Moving from left to right, the mural depicts early Basque explorers and seafarers who crossed the ocean to the Americas, a rural *baserri* (Basque farmhouse), a snippet of Pablo Picasso's mural "Guernica" about the 1937 bombing of Gernika, and the "Tree of Gernika" that withstood the bombing in front of the Basque Parliament. The landscape moves from the lush green and sea of the Basque Country to the golden Boise foothills to a high desert sheepcamp. The Uberuaga-Aguirre Star boardinghouse and St. John's Cathedral frame ghostlike Juanita Uberuaga Hormaechea, the "mother" of Boise's Basque dancers, who appears behind Boise's Oinkari Basque Dancers. Musical giant Jimmy Jausoro and weight-lifter Jose Luis Arrieta represent the Basque love of music and sports.

Viewers get a full picture of the Basque journey through time — *and place* — with this Egungoak piece of art. It's a stunning tribute to the shaping of Basque-American identity in the American West.

Conclusion

In summary, Egungoak efforts toward Basque cultural persistence demonstrate outward ethnic expression, and conscious choice to preserve culture, with an emphasis on education as a central tool. The places of this generation reveal the evolution of outward Basque ethnic expression, and its effect on their places, many of which are operating today as educational institutions.

The shift from the internal ethnic expression of the Amerikanuak supported sociologist Marcus Lee Hansen's statement, "What the son [of immigrants] wishes to forget, the grandson wishes to remember."[54] It also aligned with Herbert Gan's "symbolic identity" principle with outward expression, and demonstrated Mary Waters's theory that later descendants of immigrant generations in America actively chose their ethnicity.

The Basque Museum and Cultural Center can be viewed as the Basque Block's cultural anchor, an educational institution with a mission to "preserve, promote, and perpetuate Basque culture."[55] This is where the foundation is laid for cultural understanding and historical context. The Anduiza Fronton stands in tribute to the Basque national sport, and to the only distinctive Old World Basque architectural structure that stands in America. The Basque Center facelift demonstrated public recognition of homeland culture amid the greater American society on the heels of a dual generation that did not always publicly express ethnicity. The Unmarked Basque Graves Projects pay homage to all those who made the courageous decision to build lives in America, far from their homeland. This project also demonstrates respect for those who worked hard on American soil and may not have had family or friends to send their souls "home," where the cemetery was their final connection to their ancestors. The Boiseko Ikastola is testament to Basque cultural persistence of the future. Boise's Basque mural demonstrates that *place* mattered to this ethnic group's cultural establishment, growth, and maintenance, whether in the homeland or in the American West.

Each of these Basque places represent the Egungoak element of conscious choice to actively and publicly express culture. The Egungoak epitomizes the Bieter's "Ethnic Generation" construct because they are largely responsible for sustaining Basque culture in a public manner, where "choosing to be Basque" is an element of cultural persistence. Symbolic ethnicity (as described by Gans) is not only alive and well, but it is thriving on Grove Street, in Basque cultural festivals, and in various Basque educational efforts today. The Basque Block is loaded with ethnic symbolism.

EGUNGOAK

Clearly, the Egungoak have reached Jean Phinney's stage of ethnic identity development that is secure in its expression and achievement. The places of the Egungoak support Carmelo Urza's accurate assessment of the contemporary "Post-Modern Age of Institutions," through the success of the Basque Museum and Cultural Center, Boiseko Ikastola preschool, and Boise State University's Basque Studies Program. However, in contrast to Douglass's assertion that the Egungoak are "culture seekers," these examples instead contend that Egungoak are, in lines with the terms of Waters, the Bieters, and even Gans, "culture choosers."

Douglass also once asserted that the Basques have "contributed little to the landscape in the form of bricks and mortar."[56] While this statement was made in 1992, prior to the development of Boise's Basque Block with restaurants, a market, and large-scale events, the preservation of the Jacobs boardinghouse, the reclamation of the Anduiza Fronton, or the permanent Ikastola school in Boise, it still does not exactly reflect the Boise experience.

Frontons were distinctive Basque structures that were transplanted from the Old Country throughout the American West, and Boise had four. The Anduiza Fronton celebrated its hundredth anniversary, another testament to the power of Basque people and place. It could also be suggested that although Boise's Basque Center is not a reproduction of a baserri or any other homeland structure, it is a brick-and-mortar structure, built by Basques, for Basques, on the American landscape.

The Egunoak contributions to both the places and people of Boise are numerous and significant through time. The evolution of places from the boardinghouse to the Basque Block demonstrates the parallel evolution of Basque ethnic expression that ultimately leads to the conclusion that Basque culture persists today in Boise. The public expression of ethnic identity did not herald the decline of ethnicity as Gans and Alba predicted. Rather, the Boise case study demonstrates a sustained display of cultural diversity, and it appears to be vibrantly moving forward.

Tara Eiguren, owner of the Basque Market, pours txakoli for customers. Photo courtesy Meggan Laxalt Mackey.

CHAPTER 4 – LAU
AURRERA – MOVING FORWARD

Basque Center sign. Original photo courtesy Allan Ansell Photography. Digital photo illustration by Meggan Laxalt Mackey.

LEKUAK: THE BASQUE PLACES OF BOISE, IDAHO

Bar Gernika has been sharing Basque food on Boise's Basque Block since 1991. Photo Meggan Laxalt Mackey.

CHAPTER 4 – LAU ‖ AURRERA
Moving Forward

The Boisetarrak are not stuck in the past, and they certainly don't spend all their time paying homage to their ancestors. This is an active community. The Boise Basques have managed to keep Basque feelings and traditions alive thanks to the tenacity of hundreds of volunteers who have taken it upon themselves to pass on to the next generation the legacy their parents handed down to them.

Iñaki Aguirre Arizmendi, General Secretary of Foreign Action
for the Basque Government in Euskadi

LEKUAK BEGAN WITH A VISIT TO BOISE'S BASQUE BLOCK, THE ONLY DISTRICT IN THE UNITED STATES DEDICATED TO BASQUE CULTURE. Basque places that have existed in Boise for over a hundred years stand as testament to the legacy of generations of Basques. It is fitting that *Lekuak*, a book about *places*, should conclude with a return journey to the Basque Block. As Iñaki Aguirre Arizmendi observed, Basque identity has evolved through time, people, and place. On the Basque Block, the evolution of Basque culture through at least three generations is observable and palpable. Boise Basques are now challenged to passing this cultural legacy along to the next generations as they move forward (*aurrera*).

A visitor can experience several generations' places on this one Block: the Cyrus Jacobs-Uberuaga boardinghouse, the Anduiza Fronton, the Basque Center, and the Basque Museum and Cultural Center. Contemporary places of Basque culture contribute to this ethnic experience, such as Bar Gernika, the Basque Market, and Leku Ona restaurant and hotel. A person can also observe Basque culture from a walk on the Block without setting a foot in any of those places, largely because of the visible symbols on the streetscape. It is possible to see the nexus of immigrant and contemporary Basque generations when Euskara is spoken, traditional dance and music are performed, and educational programs are conducted.

LEKUAK: THE BASQUE PLACES OF BOISE, IDAHO

The Basque Block: Public Cultural Expression

In a little more than a hundred years, Boise's Grove Street has evolved from an internally-focused ethnic community of the Amerikanuak generation into the Basque Block, a place of public cultural expression. The foundational principle of auzolan, or communal work, is critical to the history of Boise's Basque places. There is a Basque saying, "*Indarrak biltruk obro doke ezik barriatruk,*" which means "the sum of the strengths is greater than each individually." That is what Auzolan is. It helped the Amerikanuak generation survive economically, socially, and culturally in a new place far from Euskal Herria. Auzolan was the only way the Tartekoak could have built the Basque Center. Egungoak Basques joined forces with the larger non-Basque community, again with auzolan, to create the Basque Block.

The Basque Block is a story of the evolution of people and place, and conscious choice to preserve Basque culture in Boise. Basques Adelia Garro Simplot and Rich Hormaechea invested in historic properties at 607, 611, 619, and Bar Gernika (former Cub Bar) throughout the 1980s and 1990s, which set the precedence for cultural preservation efforts on Grove Street. The Basque Neighborhood Marketplace, Inc. organization followed on those efforts with their 1987 push to preserve historic Basque buildings farther on Grove Street.[1] In 1988, this influenced the City of Boise to task Jerome Mapp with developing a master plan for the renovation of Grove Street, including a concept for an open-air market that would draw more non-Basque visitors to this part of the city.[2]

The Basque Block was completed in 2000, just in time for Jaialdi. It is the only cultural district dedicated to Basque culture in the United States. Photo courtesy Basque Museum and Cultural Center, Boise, Idaho.

The next ten years indicated growing support for a Basque district on Grove Street, with dual purposes: to preserve Basque culture and to support the city's economic development. By the 1990s, it appeared that both goals were reasonable and attainable. Interest in the Basque community increased, as the 1990 and 1995 Jaialdi celebrations demonstrated with large crowds that visited Boise for the cultural events. The idea to create a Basque cultural district on Grove Street gained solid traction by 1999. Capitol City Development Corporation (CCDC) pledged over a hundred thousand dollars, and business owners on Grove Street (the Basque organizations, Bar Gernika, Heath's Business Interiors of Idaho, and Bar de Nay) collectively committed one hundred thousand in funding, plus in-kind contributions.[3] The City of Boise added a hundred thousand, and the Ada County Highway District (ACHD), contributed another fifty thousand.[4]

In January of 1999, the Basque community and the City of Boise suffered a tremendous blow. Pat and Eloise Garmendia Bieter, Boiseans who had dedicated years of service to Basque culture and education, were tragically killed in an auto accident. This terrible event galvanized Boiseans into action to transform tragedy into what would become a source of ethnic and civic pride for the city. The City's Visual Arts Advisory Committee appropriated twenty-eight thousand dollars, and earmarked a public art project as part of the Grove Street beautification plan in honor of the Bieters.[5] That was the magic touch, and from that point forward, Basques and non-Basques committed untold hours to reshape Grove Street into the Basque Block.

The laiak entry sculptures were designed by Boise artist Ward P. Hooper in honor of Pat and Eloise Bieter. Photo courtesy Basque Museum and Cultural Center, Boise, Idaho.

AURRERA
Moving Forward (The Future)

• **The Basque Block**
Public Cultural Expression

• **Preserving Culture**
Basque Places in the
Twenty-First Century

LEKUAK: THE BASQUE PLACES OF BOISE, IDAHO

The Basque Block was a risk. It also was a demonstration of the significance of cultural diversity in America — and how inclusion, not exclusion, produces a greater whole for everyone in a community. The official grand opening of Boise's new Basque Block occurred on July 28, 2000 during the international Jaialdi celebration.[6] Thousands of people, Basque and non-Basque, attended the event, and a delegation from the Basque Government also traveled to Boise for the opening. The project was widely supported by the public. This contemporary cultural district was a first for the American West. No other community in the United States has developed a comparable Basque place.

The Basque Block reveals the evolution of the Basques through time in Boise. It is comprised of Basque places that represent each generation, such as the Amerikanuak Cyrus Jacobs-Uberuaga boardinghouse, the Tartekoak Basque Center, and the Egungoak Basque Museum. The Block reflects each generation's commitment to community, and to the communal spirit that moves not only the Basques, but Boise and its visitors, forward today.

In 2000 the Bieters analyzed the third generation's choice to return to their ancestral roots, noting it "fulfilled both the need for a unique identity and the simultaneous desire to be part of a community."[7] Both unique identity and community are hallmarks of the Basque Block, evidenced by the sharing of ancestral culture through language, food, dance, symbols, and education, for everyone.

Clearly this is not a return to older eras or a re-creation of days past. Rather, the Basque Block embodies Herbert Gans's principle of *symbolic ethnicity*: it is the Egungoak way of publicly expressing ethnic identity, with pride.

Multiple Basque generations frequent the Basque Block for socializing, learning, and sharing. Basque Center photo courtesy Erin Ann Jensen. Basque Market photo courtesy Meggan Laxalt Mackey.

AURRERA

"Given identity" focused the immigrant Amerikanuak inward, knowing ethnicity was "a legacy that we received at birth, without seeking it or working for it, and it is not sufficient for us to tacitly fail to accept it."[8] The Cyrus Jacobs-Uberuaga boardinghouse and Anduiza Fronton symbolize the legacy of the Amerikanuak generation, and their places, which aided the immigrant transition. Undeniably, Amerikanuak places resulted from given identity. The Tartekoak Basque Center represents the beginning of a transition from given identity to *chosen identity*. This place, originally intended for solely Basque purpose and function, evolved into a place that expressed the dual identity of being Basque *and* American. The Basque Museum is an Egungoak-created educational institution, the result of later generations actively choosing to maintain their culture. Museum membership, exhibits, and educational programs directly connect Basques to their heritage and also expand the cultural reach beyond the inner Basque circle.

Basque symbols on the Basque Block serve as visible connections to homeland culture. This is true to Gans's concept of symbolic ethnicity. The imposing *laiak* are symbols of Basque strength and hard work. The oak tree at the Cyrus Jacobs-Uberuaga boardinghouse is a sapling from the real *Gernikako Arbola* (Oak Tree of Gernika), which signifies ancient Basque laws (*foruak*) that gave all citizens the right to self-determination, autonomy, and freedom.[9] Ikurrina flags fly everywhere. The sidewalks symbolize permanence, as lauburus, family surnames, songs, and seven Zazpiak Bat coats of arms stand in granite and concrete for all to see.

Around the corner from Bar Gernika, the Basque mural represents the transition from Old Country to New World. This public art depicts Basque migration to the American West, but ultimately, it symbolizes something greater. It tells the tale of a culture that has persisted

The Egungoak generation has achieved cultural preservation through various educational means. Photos courtesy Meggan Laxalt Mackey.

through courage, self-determination, and cultural expression. The Block's interpretive signs offer bits and pieces of history and culture to passersby, not only as an outward display of culture, but in an effort to educate. Basque food and drink on the Basque Block can also be considered symbolic ethnicity, especially considering the traditional meals and customs that the Basques still maintain today. Dances, concerts, Basque bands, and festivals such as San Inazio and Jaialdi fall in this same category.

Symbolic ethnicity is alive and well on Boise's Basque Block. It is as much a reminder of singular Old World culture as it heralds a new future of plurality. Non-Basques can share in Basque celebrations, food, and other customs. Conversely, visitors to the Block can also patronize non-Basque businesses and events. Non-Basque businesses support Basques by their presence on the Block, and their fiscal commitment is integral to the thriving downtown district known as the Basque Block.

The Basque Block represents the importance of ethnic place in contemporary times. It contributes economically, socially, and culturally to the City of Boise. Several Basque places converge here, exposing the evolution from internally focused boardinghouses and frontons to externally shared public spaces. It is rare to find multiple generational places that are highly visible in one spot.

Boise's Basque Block demonstrates the persistence of Basque culture in the twenty-first century. It signals a greater appreciation for and acceptance of ethnic expression today, not a decline of ethnicity. A newspaper editorial in the *Caldwell Tribune-Idaho Free Press* once observed Basque ethnicity and its impact on American society, "Basque blood runs strong, even in the second and third generations. A Basque will always be a Basque — proud, vigorous, and self-confident — even if he is an American. And America is so much richer for it." [10]

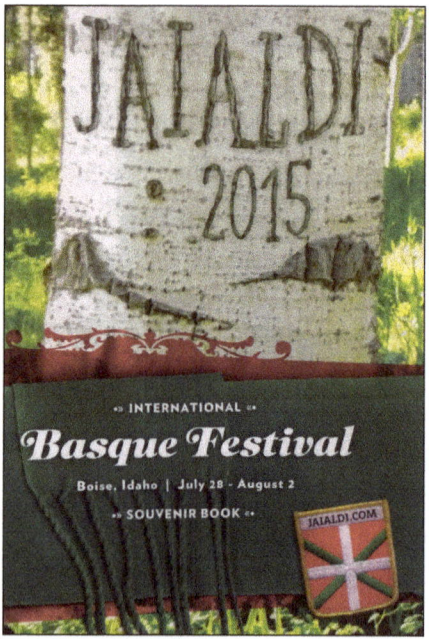

Jaialdi 2015 program booklet. Photo courtesy Meggan Laxalt Mackey.

AURRERA

Preserving Culture: Basque Places in the Twenty-First Century

This book focuses on the persistence of Basque culture through *place*. It traces how Basque places reflect the evolution of each generation's expression of ethnic identity in response to American societal forces through time. It applies the lens of place to the case study of Basques in Boise, Idaho, to document the cultural persistence of this ethnic group for over a hundred years. Place is seen as a valid construct from which culture can be examined. It is precisely the intersection of people and place through time that allows for this rich investigation.

History tells us much about the past, and it can guide us into the future. Scholars have contributed to studies of Basques in the American West for over sixty years.[11] *Lekuak* supports, challenges, and extends the work of Basque scholars John Bieter, Mark Bieter, Carmelo Urza, and William Douglass, who have used generational, institutional, and societal parameters to examine Basque culture.

In 2000, Basque historians and brothers John and Mark Bieter published a pivotal book, *An Enduring Legacy: The Story of Basques in Idaho*. The book was organized by successive generations: the "immigrant," "hyphenated," and "ethnic generations." *An Enduring Legacy* expanded the story of Basques in the American West by shifting the story of immigration and assimilation into the sphere of sociology, based on sociologist Marcus Lee Hansen's "third generation theory" that ethnic revival occurred with the third [Basque] generation.[12] The co-authors conclude with *The Ethnic Generation's* symbolic ethnicity and "choosing to be Basque" as potential pillars of Basque cultural persistence into the future. That was year 2000.

Eighteen years later, *Lekuak* extends the Bieters' conclusion: "What cultural traits survive and what new ones will be created depend, as always, on the choices the late generations make."[13] Since 2000, Basques in Boise have chosen to preserve their culture through innovation, multiculturalism, and increasingly public demonstrations of ethnicity. Place has been central to these choices, impacting Basques in the United States, the diaspora, and the Basque Country.

Scores of immigrant Basque men worked as sheepherders in the high desert ranges and mountains of the American West. Arborglyphs are remnants of the places where Amerikanuak herders earned a living. Photo courtesy Meggan Laxalt Mackey.

LEKUAK: THE BASQUE PLACES OF BOISE, IDAHO

Consider the *Jaialdi* celebrations that have exploded exponentially from 2000 to the last 2015 event: thousands of attendees from across the world have chosen to attend this celebration of Basque culture in Boise every five years. In 2015, record numbers streamed to the Basque Block and the Idaho fairgrounds for Jaialdi. Thousands that same summer to watch the first-ever Basque Soccer Friendly game between *La Liga's Athletic Club de Bilbao* and *Liga MX's Club Tijuana Xoloitzcuintles de Caliente* at Boise State University. Boise Basques Argia Beristain Dougherty, John Bieter, and others accomplished this remarkable effort, and succeeded at the transformation of Boise State's infamous artificial blue turf into real green grass for the international soccer game.

The Basque Museum and Cultural Center membership in 2018 is not far from 1000, and its annual visitorship has grown to almost 18,000 since the museum has significantly expanded on-site collections, exhibits, educational programs, website, and public events like WineFest and Running of the Bars[14] Museum volunteer rolls have steadily increased to meet the demand for tours of the museum and its Cyrus Jacobs-Uberuaga boardinghouse, Anduiza Fronton, and Basque Mural — all on the Basque Block. Persons of many cultures are enrolled in Euskara classes at the museum year after year, with a solid core of Egungoak and later-generations of Basques committed to learning their ancient language.

The Anduiza Fronton celebrated its hundred-year anniversary in 2014 with growing numbers of local and traveling players who compete in tournaments throughout the year. The same for players ranging across many generations who compete in the Basque card game *mus*, usually in the upstairs card room at the Basque Center. The Basque Center is continuously booked full with Basque and non-Basque community events and its membership now nudges 1100 members.[15] Dance and music have also mushroomed far beyond the 2000 entertainment scene, led by the *Oinkari Basque Dancers*, the very popular band *Amuma Says No,* and the *Txantxangorriak* group, formed by Boise teacher and restauranteur Dan Ansotegui, is now comprised of a bulging number of *triki trixa* (accordion) and *pandareta* (tambourine) players, including youth as young as eight years old. The *Biotzetik Basque Choir*, established in 1986 by Ted Totorica, now has the largest group ever, comprised of Basque and non-Basque singers. This choir spreads Basque musical heritage worldwide, including performances at the 2016 *Smithsonian Institution's Folklife Festival* on the National Mall.

Most significantly, since the publication of *An Enduring Legacy*, Boise's Basque Block has grown to bea seminal place for those of Basque ancestry to express their ethnic heritage — and it also is primary downtown cultural district for locals and visitors of *any* ethnic heritage. It is the culmination of symbolic ethnicity and multiculturalism. The Basque Block confirms that since *Enduring Legacy* was published, significant choices have been made by to preserve Basque culture in many ways, and in many places. *Egungoak* places such as the Basque Museum, Boiseko Ikastola, and Boise State University's Basque Studies program demonstrate that learning at all ages is critical to cultural understanding. *Lekuak* takes the well-documented study of the Bieters eighteen years further, peering into possible reasons how Egungoak revived Basque culture through place.

Biozetik Basque Choir, Txantxangorriak, Boise Oinkari Dancers with Dan Ansotegui, and packed houses for educational events at the Basque Museum and Basque Center. Photos courtesy respective Basque organizations' promotional materials and websites.

LEKUAK: THE BASQUE PLACES OF BOISE, IDAHO

The Amerikanuak generation reflects, in the words of renowned Basque scholar and anthropologist William Douglass, immigrants who traveled "straight from the Pyrenees with no need to step outside an established Basque network."[16] The boardinghouses, frontons, and the Church of the Good Shepherd demonstrated that first-generation Basques were in survival mode, highly dependent on one another, who used their internal ethnic networks to maintain social cohesion. Their places ensured cultural safety.

In addition, Douglass characterized the American-born children of immigrants as "rejectors" of their Old World heritage, language, customs, and politics. These Tartekoak generation members were "in-between" being Basque and American. Places such as residences in suburban neighborhoods, Basque businesses that had American names, and temporary gathering places indicate the Tartekoak did not display the solely-Basque ethnicity of their parents, but instead, a hybrid Basque-American identity. This becomes evident when examining this generation's places. By the end of the Tartekoak period, Boise's Basques had built the Basque Center, clearly a move to openly express their ethnic heritage through the deliberate construction of the Basque social hall in town, a permanent structure. This was a transformation of place due to its permanence.

Douglass identified the third generation, what is known in *Lekuak* as Egungoak, as Basque culture "seekers."[17] The Egungoak generation's places confirm Douglass' belief that these members deliberately sought the ethnic heritage of their ancestors, and then displayed it whenever possible in many places. The Egungoak sought to learn through a multitude of educational methods and they connected symbolically with their heritage. Though some structures are from periods long ago, the adaptive re-use of these places by a willing collective essentially constitutes a new place, such as Boise's Basque Block.

While it is generally true that although Basques had a longtime presence in the American West, they did not alter the landscape in any large-scale physical manner.[18] William Douglass stated this observation in the 1992 publication of *To Build in a New Land: Ethnic Landscapes in North America*, "If we pose the question of what kind of ethnic mark the Basque-American community has implanted upon the [architectural] landscape of the American West, the answer must be, practically none... The Basques contributed little to the American landscape in the form of bricks and mortar."[19]

The Boise experience challenges Douglass's assertion however, because some Basque places, though sometimes not originally Basque-built but were later adapted to Basque uses, such as historic boardinghouses, still stand as part of the landscape in the American West. Although Basque places in America rarely looked like those of the homeland, their functions connected Basques symbolically to ancestral memory, which did result in some visible "bricks and mortar" contributions to Boise's landscape. Several Boise structures can be considered to be contributions to ethnic landscapes, certainly in the west: historic boardinghouses (six still stand today in Boise, with the Cyrus Jacobs-Uberuaga as the only fully restored), frontons (open-air remnants and the indoor Anduiza Fronton), and the Basque Center. The Church of the Good Shepherd still stands as a tangible structure once used by Basques, but it has long been a non-religious facility. The Basque Block has become a cultural district, comprised of several historic and post-modern buildings under adaptive reuse. In its entirety, the Block as a whole is a tangible contribution to the landscape, though not one bricks and mortar structure.

The generation-by-generation examination of Boise's Basque places parallels Jean Phinney's assertions that ethnic identity develops through time.[20] The Basque places also evolve, from first-generation places of birth or given identity such as boardinghouses; to the second generation places that reflect dual ethnic identity as with the Basque Center; and finally to the third generation's Basque Block.

Boise's Basque Block contains Herbert Gans's ethnicity elements: ethnic organizations and institutions that are promotional, commercial, performing, preserving; private ethnic practices; and outward expression of ethnic identity.[21] All of these elements appear in Boise's Basque places today, well-positioned to continue into the future. The Basque Block is the pinnacle of Gans' outward expression of ethnic identity.

Places of education, performance, and faith are familiar to those who share in Basque culture today. Photos courtesy Meggan Laxalt Mackey.

Lastly, there is a cornerstone element to consider: the third generation's conscious choice to express ethnic identity in public places. Sociologist Mary Waters posited that ethnic groups in America today have choice of ethnic identification, as well as choice to demonstrate ethnicity publicly. Waters claimed that the combination of involuntary heredity and personal choice allows for the individual expression of ethnic identity, which ultimately leads to "pride of heritage and pluralist values of diversity."[22]

LEKUAK: THE BASQUE PLACES OF BOISE, IDAHO

Boise's Basque places demonstrate diversity through the manifestation of choice to "be Basque," particularly with the Egungoak generation's deliberate expression of symbolic ethnicity. This can be seen in Egungoak expression of outward symbols, such as icons, cultural festivals, food, language, dance, music, and educational institutions that are highly visible on the Basque Block.

Ethnicity is foundational in defining American identity: "more than ever, to be American is defined as being an immigrant or the descendant of an immigrant, and this reinforces people's links with their immigrant pasts."[23] The Basque Block is one link of a particular ethnic group's immigrant past. It stands strong as an ultimate symbol of ethnicity, a tribute to the foundation of America's multicultural identity. This is the power of the intersection of Basque people and place through time.

POSTSCRIPT
WHY BOISE?

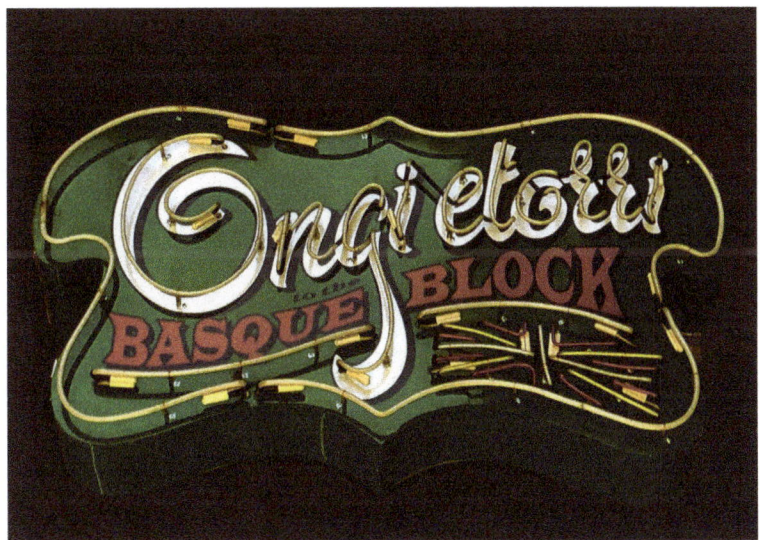

Ongi Etorri ("Welcome") - a Basque greeting appears in downtown Boise's transit center across from the Basque Block near the Boise Centre convention area. Photo courtesy Meggan Laxalt Mackey.

SOME HAVE ASKED, "WHY BOISE?" "What is the 'special sauce' for Basque preservation in Boise in the twenty-first century?" This book's sociological and historical frameworks partly answer these questions. A short examination of additional factors, however, may provide some interesting thoughts to consider. None are conclusive, and all are matter of opinion rather than absolute fact. Taken together though, demographics, economics, discrimination, and ties between Boise and the Basque Country may form a more comprehensive answer as to why Basque culture remains strong in Boise today.

LEKUAK: THE BASQUE PLACES OF BOISE, IDAHO

Jaialdi has become the main Basque festival in the United States since it was celebrated in 1987 in Boise ... What was first organized as a Basque-American festival has now evolved into an international event, to which thousands of visitors are attracted, not only from the United States, but from many other countries in the whole Basque diaspora. Only Boise could organize such a terrific event ...

The tradition of the "Auzolan," which was the basis of the cooperative being of the Basque farmers and has spotted our cooperative industry making us unique in the world, can be portrayed now in the organization and celebration of Basque Culture in Boise. That is the key for the preservation of our identity.

Lehendakari Iñigo Urkullu Renteria, Welcome Address to Boise for *Jaialdi* 2015

POSTSCRIPT

Demographics

The Basque population in Boise is perceived to be substantial. The Basque Block is flourishing, thousands attend Boise's Basque festivals, and it sometimes seems like every fifth person in the city is Basque, or knows a Basque. Also, Boise is the only place in the United States that has dedicated an entire city block to Basque culture. In 2000, the U.S Census counted 6,637 persons of Basque ancestry in Idaho out of 57,793 Basques nationally.[1] By 2014, anecdotal estimates tally Boise's population between seven and ten thousand people, or about 3.2 percent of the city's overall population of 216,282, which indicates there is a high concentration of Basques in a relatively small geographic area.[2] Comparatively in Nevada, 6,096 Basques were counted among an overall population of 236,995 people, or a little more than 2.5 percent of the total population, dispersed across an expansive statewide landscape.[3] The largest concentration of Basques in a western town, however, is in Winnemucca, Nevada, where Basques comprise 4.2 percent of the total citywide population of eight thousand.[4] Possible speculations as to why cultural persistence appears to be stronger in Boise, Idaho, may be that when ethnic groups are concentrated in smaller regions geographically such as Boise or Winnemucca, as opposed to being dispersed across a larger region like San Francisco, or if dense clustering occurs in enclave-type neighborhoods or in public spaces such as the Basque Block, the relatively larger presence is more outwardly visible.

Basques have been clustered near Grove Street throughout Boise's history, as evidenced by living, work, and worship places that were first formed near the downtown center of business and state government. Other ethnic groups though, including large numbers of documented Irish, Greeks, Chinese, Germans, and Jews also lived, worked, worshiped, and recreated in the city, but they either moved away from or did not remain near the downtown center of commerce for as long as the Basques, who were more concentrated in Boise's Grove Street and North End areas.[5]

Some members of another ethnic group, the African-Americans, settled near Boise's River and Ash neighborhood from the late 1800s through early 1900s.[6] This was near the south side of the railroad tracks, a section of clear racial and class divide. This distinctly segregated settlement was home to many of Boise's minority groups, including a few Basques. Throughout Boise's history, there have always been fewer Blacks than Basques, as can be seen by the 2014 population estimate of 3,043 African-Americans in the city, or 1.5 percent of the total population.[7]

Another possible demographic consideration is that Boise is the capital city of Idaho. Basques have almost always been a few steps away from the Idaho Statehouse. Close proximity to lawmakers in the seat of government has allowed Basques to influence state and city economic and social infrastructure, and to contribute to national state, city, and county government. Basques in Boise have a history of political and civic involvement, influencing immigration, economics, trade, social issues, education, cultural exchanges, and city development. Basques have served in elected positions as well, including Pete Cenarrusa, who was Idaho's longest-serving elected politician for fifty-two years in the legislature and as Idaho secretary of state; Ben Ysursa, another Basque who followed Cenarrusa as Idaho secretary of state; J. Patrick Bieter, Idaho house of representatives; and David Bieter, who served in his late father's State of Idaho house seat, and has been Boise's 54th mayor since 2003. During the 2005 Jaialdi celebration, Mayor Bieter paid tribute to Boise's sister city, Gernika, indicative of international government ties:

> In 1992, the City of Boise established a sister city relationship with a town that is very close to the hearts of many in Boise: Gernika, Bizkaia. Over 100 years ago, the first immigrants from the Basque Country came to the Treasure Valley to make their way in the new world. These Basque settlers came from different towns in the Basque Country, many coming at the behest of a family member who told them work was available in Idaho. Although these men and women came from many different towns Lekeitio, Aulestia, Mundaka to name a few, virtually every Basque immigrant who came to the Boise area was born within a 30-mile radius of the City of Gernika. But the City of Gernika has even greater than a geographic significance to the Basques in Boise and around the world. Gernika is where Basque leaders, in an early example of proportional representation, met to discuss issues under the Tree of Gernika, and where the kings and queens of Spain affirmed their commitment to Basque Autonomy. How fitting, then, that the City of Trees and the town of the Tree of Gernika have become sister cities... And so we come here today to reaffirm our sister city relationship; to renew our commitment to strengthen our cultural, educational, and governmental ties.[8]

It can be surmised that demographic factors, including a concentrated settlement of Basques in a small geographic area with a sphere of political influence in close proximity to Idaho's State Capitol and City Hall have probably influenced cultural persistence in Boise.

POSTSCRIPT

Economics

Ever since the Amerikanuak era of Basque boardinghouses, Grove Street has been a place where Basques have lived, worked, and shared their culture — internally and externally. Business endeavors, however, may be able to lay claim to influencing the sustainability of Basque culture in Boise. Across the United States, shoppers patronize ethnic places such as "Little Italy" restaurants, "Little Tokyo" flower markets, and "Chinatown" shops and restaurants. There is little doubt that the economics of cultural tourism can affect the persistence of ethnic groups.

Economics play a key role in the stability of the Basque Block, and the City of Boise. Since 2000, the city and county in turn, have supported the Basque Block through grants, public programs, street development, property maintenance, and city-hosted events.[9] Basque Museum and Cultural Center executive director Annie Gavica noted that the 2015 Jaialdi festival was a spectacular tourist draw to various places in Boise, beyond the Basque Block, "At the fairgrounds for that weekend, there were 20,000 tickets used to get in, 5,000 tickets sold at Sports Night, 2,000 tickets sold for *Festara* at the Morrison Center, and an innumerable number of people on the Basque Block at all times. This was the biggest Jaialdi yet, both in numbers of people and amount of money raised."[10] Annual Basque events, such as the San Inazio festival, the museum's WineFest, and the Basque Center's Sheepherder's Ball draw thousands more to the Basque Block. Countless organizations host conferences, meetings, and other events on the Basque Block, resulting in an economic ripple effect for hotel rooms, conference spaces, restaurants, and bars. No doubt the city reaps economic benefits from Basque tourism, and vice-versa. This symbiotic effect may support cultural persistence.

In 2015, Idaho Governor Butch Otter and the Basque Autonomous Government *Lehendakari* (president) Iñigo Urkullu Renteria met to discuss international trade. Otter remarked, "The cultural heritage of the Basque people in Idaho is an integral part of who we are as a state. I am honored to welcome President Urkullu and his delegation as we look for ways to enhance our understanding and our appreciation for one another, as well as promote our shared economic interests."[11]

Governor C.L. "Butch" Otter and Lehendakari Iñigo Urkullu. Photo courtesy Spokesman-Review online, Jon Hanion.

LEKUAK: THE BASQUE PLACES OF BOISE, IDAHO

Another economic consideration is considerable financial support from Basques themselves in support of cultural preservation. Adelia Garro Simplot and Rich Hormaechea provided funding for the acquisition of several historic buildings on Grove Street, setting the foundation for the development of the Basque Block. This enabled a solid geographic base of multiple buildings that few ethnic groups in Boise can claim, except for perhaps the Jewish and Greek communities. The Basque Museum and Cultural Center relies on membership dues, fund raisers, and philanthropic giving programs to aid cultural efforts, important economic considerations for non-profit organizations. Basques also support charitable giving through museum memorials and special Basque projects such as the Community History program. Basques are their own best customers, often supporting the museum's gift shop and Basque Market. Membership dues at Boise's Basque Center provide an opportunity for Basques to support their culture in a central gathering spot, contributing fiscally to liquor sales at the bar, monthly dinners, and fund raisers. Of course, a diverse base of non-Basques also support the Center's liquor sales and facility rentals. Lastly, Basques give to educational efforts at both the Basque Museum and Cultural Center and Boise State's Basque Studies Program. Non-Basque support to cultural efforts should never be underestimated, either.

Other Basque communities in the American West support similar places, organizations, and institutions. For instance, the University of Nevada, Reno's William A. Douglass Center for Basque Studies and Reno's Monument to the Basque Sheepherder ("Solitude"), Zazpiak Bat dancers, and Basque restaurants. Reno does not, however, have a Basque Center. It is possible that these Centers provide cohesive unifying places, both socially and economically, which may bring economic support to Basques in specific geographic areas.

The role of food is central to Basque culture. Basque eateries serve thousands on and off the Basque Block. Basque food is a solid contributor to Boise's already-seismic gastronomic scene, and Boise has the largest number of food spots in one concentrated area in the United States. Culinary experts Dan Ansotegui (Bar Gernika and Basque Market founder, and manager of the Modern Hotel's *Txikiteo*), sisters Chris and Gina Urquidi (Epi's Meridian), Chef Jesus Alcelay (Basque Center and Cottonwood

Basque Museum events and gift shop sales help support cultural persistence in Boise. Photos courtesy Meggan Laxalt Mackey.

POSTSCRIPT

Grille), Tony and Tara Eiguren (Basque Market), Jeff and Stephanie May, (Bar Gernika proprietors), Bardenay President and CEO Kevin Settles, and José Maria Artiach (*Leku Ona*) work to to ensure not only good food, but Basque culture, survives in Boise.

Albertsons grocery stores inked a deal with the Basque Market to offer their specialty food and other goods on store shelves at their Broadway store, not too far from the Basque Block, which will expose shoppers to Basque culture and hopefully, will improve profit margins. The same can be said for many Basque eateries in towns small and large across the American West. Wherever they are, restaurants, bars, markets and fair booths remain the most visible (and shareable) elements of Basque culture today.

The Ysursa family had the right idea when they opened the doors of their Valencia boardinghouse to all Boiseans for good food. Indeed, food is a significant influence on Basque cultural persistence, and it is an economic mainstay in Boise.

Lastly, a core consideration in Basque cultural persistence is non-Basque contributions to efforts, small and large. "Being Basque" is not just for those of Basque descent, as Marty Peterson confirmed this a 2015 City Club of Boise luncheon, "During Jaialdi, everyone's a little bit Basque ..."[12] More than twenty-thousand attendees agreed, as they opened wallets in restaurants, at street dances, in bars, at the Basque Museum, and the Basque Soccer Friendly game between the Basque *La Liga Athletic Bilbao* and Mexico's *Liga MX Club Tijuana*.[13]

Basque delicacies, spices, and wine are in ample supply for shoppers at the Basque Market and Albertsons grocery store in Boise. Photos courtesy Meggan Laxalt Mackey.

LEKUAK: THE BASQUE PLACES OF BOISE, IDAHO

Discrimination

Despite the bright story of the Basques in Boise, or the American West for that matter, the story has not always been positive. *Lekuak* can not ignore the role of racial discrimination in the Basque-American, and other ethnic groups' history. Boise's Chinatown area once harbored temples and shops, but it was exterminated by racism during the city's urban renewal period.[14] The Morris Hill Cemetery also has separate burial areas for Chinese-Americans, serving as a painful reminder of the 1882 Chinese Exclusion Act and the Immigration Act of 1924, which prohibited all immigration from Asia. These acts attempted to decrease immigration of southern Europeans and other groups. After the bombing of Pearl Harbor, Japanese-Americans were ordered from their homes, families, and jobs to live in internment camps, such as the Minidoka Camp not too far from Boise. Many African-Americans worked as laborers, domestic help, or in other occupations in early Boise, but most did not establish commercial endeavors in town.[15] Well into 2007, only 0.2 percent of Boise's businesses were African-American owned.[16] Boise records are filled with immigrant names from Ireland, Italy, Germany, and other European countries. Though most worked to define themselves as true Americans, suspicions of their intentions ran deep.

During the Amerikanuak period, Basques initially were equated to the African-Americans or the Chinese, viewed with suspicion and treated with prejudice. The Bieters recalled a 1909 *Caldwell Tribune* article about the problem of Basques in the sheep industry, "Bascos are on par with those of the Chinaman," but even worse than the Chinese, the Basques were derogatorily coined "dirty black Bascos," who were "filthy, treacherous, and meddlesome," and "unless something was done, they would make life impossible for the white man."[17]

Discrimination was not new to Basques, though. For centuries, they were recognized as "different." Fierce defenders of their homeland, the Basques protected their region between France and Spain from invaders. They were called *hasieriak*, or "mystery people." This label categorized Basques distinct and separate

Hip Sing building and apothecary, c. 1938. Online historic photo courtesy Boise State University.

POSTSCRIPT

from others, although this was linguistically true. Yet, they survived invasions and attempts to control their borders, laws, and people.

The Basques also survived one of the most oppressive persecutions of an ethnic group. Under Spanish dictator Francisco Franco from 1937 to 1975, Basques risked their lives if they spoke Euskara, raised the Basque ikurriña (flag), sang Basque songs, or taught their children in Ikastolas (preschools). Franco and Hitler joined forces in 1937 to commit a terrible act of genocide: the bombing of Gernika. On Market Day, when most of the women and children were selling and shopping, Franco and Hitler ordered bombers over the town, eradicating thousands of Basques. That was only the beginning of the Franco rule, which led the way for many Basques to be discriminated against in their own region. In fact, escaping persecution was one reason for Basque migration away from their homeland.

The bombing of Gernika, 1937. Photo courtesy Basque Museum and Cultural Center, Gernika Peace Museum images.

Possibly because some had survived discrimination, or maybe because the Basques were white Europeans, they withstood discrimination in Boise, Idaho, to become more integrated into the larger society. The transformation of the Basques from denigrated in the 1900s to a celebrated ethnic group today indicates the power of cultural heritage to persist.

Ties between Boise and the Basque Country

The first Basque Studies Program was established by Robert Laxalt in 1967 as part of the Desert Research Institute (DRI) at the University of Nevada, Reno. Dr. William Douglass served as the Program's first director, who began an earnest academic push to study the Basques. Fewer than ten years later in 1974, Dr. Pat Bieter from Boise State University established the first formal academic Basque Studies Abroad Program. Both cities shared faculty and students on this program, which proved to be foundational to establishing a long-standing relationship between the Basque Country and cities such as Reno and Boise, where large numbers of Basques lived. By the late 1990s, relations between the Basque diaspora and the homeland grew stronger, with a concerted focus on maintaining Basque culture through dedicated Basque government-funded programs in dance, music, language, economics, and education.[18]

Foundational to close relationships between Boise and the homeland was the obvious: many Basques had crossed an ocean to build new lives in the American West, and Boise was one place of settlement. The first bonds were formed through an extended network that closely connected Basques from Euskal Herria to places like New York, and then to the American West.

During the Franco period (1937-1975), the first Basque president, José Antonio Aguirre, was forced to flee the Basque Country. After taking his oath of office in 1936, Aguirre operated the goverment-in-exile from many places, including New York. The government established the "Delegation of Euskadi in America" to closely with Basques in the United States, including Boise and nearby Emmett, Idaho.

Other historic examples exist to confirm strong ties between Boise and the Basque Country, and they have grown deeper through the years. Today the ties are beyond families: they reach into civic, cultural, economic, and academic relationships, mutually benefiting Boise and the Basque Country. The Basque Autonomous Government continues to provide fiscal support to American cultural and educational institutions such as the Basque Museum and Cultural Center, and its Ikastola, Boise State University's Basque Studies Program, and community programs. The Basque Museum and Cultural Center has garnered Basque Autonomous Government fiscal support since 1996, with grants up to twenty-five thousand dollars each for Ikastola programs and educators, oral histories, exhibits and programs, equipment, and museum gallery support.[19]

Boise State University and the Etxepare Institute established the Eloise Garmendia Bieter Chair position in the Basque Studies program in 2016/2017. Iñaki Goirizalaia, then president of the University of the Basque Country (EHU) was the first Bieter Chair. Several film producers,

Lehendakari (president) José Antonio Aguirre's Basque government-in-exile delegation on the Idaho Statehouse steps. Photos courtesy Basque Museum and Cultural Center, Villanueva family collection.

POSTSCRIPT

musicians, and dance groups have formed close ties due to their Boise visits. Civic exchanges, such as when the City of Boise hosted Imanol Galdos to complete doctoral work that focused on Boise and Donostia-San Sebastián in 2018, have helped promote collaborative city government relations. The Basque Market hosts culinary tours in the Basque Country, and Basque Museum and Cultural Center staff visited Basque Country museums and cultural centers, further reinforcing these ties. Several students from the Basque Country have studied at Boise State in undergraduate and graduate programs in engineering, history, and education, and the number of Basque exchange students in Boise is at an all-time high. The Basque Museum employs interns from the Basque Country as teachers at the Ikastola, and native Basque speakers teach adult Euskara language classes each semester at the museum.

More examples abound, including support from North American Association of Basque Organizations (NABO) for cultural exchanges between the Basque Country and the diaspora. Basque Autonomous Government representatives travel to Boise to speak at special events, such as educational programs, Jaialdi, the Unmarked Graves Projects, Basque film premieres, and Boiseans travel the other direction. During the 2015 Jaialdi festival, Lehendakari (president) Iñigo Urkullu Renteria said, "Boise is the city outside of the Basque Country where the presence and Basque influence, both in politics and in culture, is felt the strongest. The cultural affinity, knowledge and respect for the Basques in Boise make this place an outstanding platform for the Basque Country in the United States."[20]

The importance of relationships between Boise and the Basque Country cannot be overemphasized. Boise Basques have cultivated and maintained relationships with their Euro-Basque counterparts for many years. The effect of strong Boise-homeland relations is a global, transnational exchange that signals a symbiotic effort to maintain Basque culture. Boise is unique in the diaspora because of places like the Basque Block and events such as Jaialdi in the city, but personal connections are more likely the truest "ties that bind."

This Postscript offers possible considerations to answer the question, "Why Boise?" Boise is by no means the sole bastion of Basque culture today in the United States, but it serves as inspiration for the future of cultural preservation.

Boise's Basque Museum and Cultural Center staff visit to the Basque Country encouraged cultural exchange. Photo courtesy Annie Gavica.

The Ysursa Family's Modern Hotel boardinghouse at 615 Idaho Street, c. 1924-1925. Photo courtesy Ysursa collection at the Basque Museum and Cultural Center, Boise, Idaho.

TIMELINE

  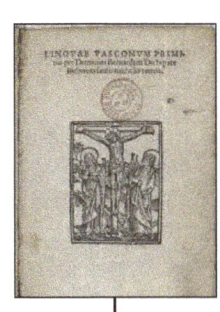

35,000 BC
Cro-Magnon Period
Basques may have
inhabited Pyrenees

1452
Basque foral law
Fuero Viejo
de Vizcaya

1500s–1800s
Basque whalers, mariners,
explorers, military,
merchants, missionaries

1545
Bernard Etxepare prints
Linguæ Vasconum Primitiæ,
first Basque book

1776
U.S. Declaration
of Independence

1789
U.S. Bill of Rights

1789–1799
French Revolution

1833–1840
First Carlist War

1846–1849
Second Carlist War

1872–1876
Third Carlist War

TIMELINE

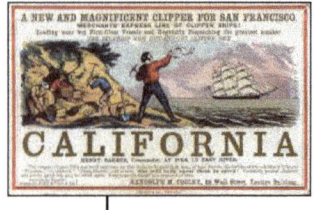   

AMERIKANUAK

1848
California Gold Rush - Basques migrate north from South Americas

1863
Fort Boise established

1864
City of Boise Incorporated; Capital of Idaho Territory

1869
Transcontinental Railroad - Basques migrate west

AMERIKANUAK

1882
Chinese Exclusion Act

1889
Silver discovered in Idaho DeLamar Mine, Silver City

1898
José Navarro and Antonio Azcuenaga arrive in Idaho

1890
Idaho Statehood; First Boise boarding-house: The Gestal/Spanish Restaurant

1895
Sabino Arana y Goiri establishes Basque Nationalist Party and creates *ikurriña* (Basque flag)

TIMELINE

AMERIKANUAK

1898
Spanish-Amerian War

1900s–1920s
First wave of immigration to U.S. through Ellis Island, New York
Large numbers of Basque men work as sheepherders in the west

1911
Aita Arregui assigned to the Basque community in Boise

1913
Valentin Aguirre forms *Centro Vasco Americano* Basque Center in New York City

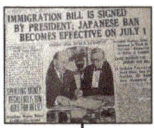

AMERIKANUAK

1914
Juan ("Big Jack") Anduiza builds boardinghouse and fronton at 619 Grove

1914–1918
World War I

1917
U.S. Immigration requires literacy

1919-1921
Boise's Basque Church of the Good Shepherd

1921
U.S. Emergency Quota Act (Immigration Restriction Act)

1924
Johnson-Reed Act

TIMELINE

AMERIKANUAK | TARTEKOAK

1929
Boise Sheepherder's Ball created by John Archabal

1929–1939
Great Depression

1934
Taylor Grazing Act

1936–1939
Spanish Civil War; 1937 Bombing of Gernika by Franco and Hitler; Basque Government-in-Exile begins

TARTEKOAK

1939–1945
World War II

1949
Boise Music Week "Song of the Basque" and Euzkaldunak, Inc. forms

1949–1950
Boise's Basque Center

1950–1953
Korean War

1955–1975
Vietnam War

114

TIMELINE

TARTEKOAK — **EGUNGOAK**

1957
Sweet Promised Land by Robert Laxalt

1959
First Basque Festival Sparks, Nevada

1960–1964
Boise Oinkari Dancers
World's Fair - Seattle (1962)
World's Fair - New York (1964)

1963
President John F. Kennedy assassinated

1968
Rev. Martin Luther King assassinated

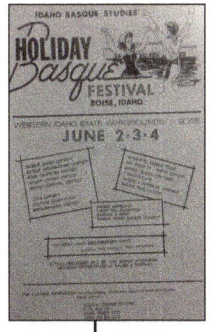    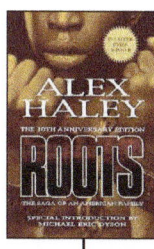

EGUNGOAK

1972
Boise Basque Studies Holiday Basque Festival; Basque Center façade

1973
North American Basque Organizations (NABO)

1974
Boise-Oñati Basque Studies Abroad Program, Dr. Pat Bieter

1975
William A. Douglass and Jon Bilbao's *Amerikanuak* published

1977
Alex Haley's *Roots* published

TIMELINE

EGUNGOAK

1983
Adelia Garro Simplot purchases 607 Grove St., Uberuaga's boardinghouse; forms Basque Cultural Center of Idaho

1985
Basque Museum formed

1987
First Jaialdi; Biotzetik Choir; Jesus Alcelay opens Oñati restaurant

1988
Adelia Garro Simplot purchases 611 Grove St for expanded museum operations; Gernika tree sapling at 607 Grove

1990–1991
Adelia Garro Simplot purchases Cub Bar; Bar Gernika; Second Boise Jaialdi festival

EGUNGOAK

1993
Adelia Garro Simplot and Rich Hormaechea purchase 1914 Anduiza Fronton bldg

1995
Jaialdi #3 in Boise

1998
Boiseko Ikastola established

1999
Home Away from Home by Jeronima Echeverria; *Portraits of Basques*, edited by Etulain and Echeverria

2000
Basque Block; Jaialdi #4; Basque Mural; *An Enduring Legacy* John/Mark Bieter

2003
Cyrus Jacobs-Uberuaga restoration

TIMELINE

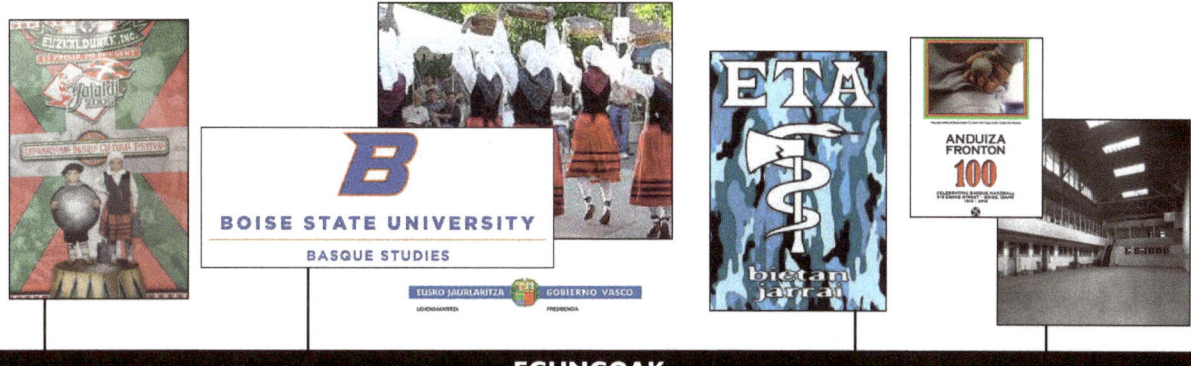

EGUNGOAK

2005
Jaialdi #5; Boise State University launches Basque Studies

2006
Basque Government begins support of educational programs in Boise museum, ikastola, university

2010
Jaialdi #6; Ellis Island tribute; *Hidden in Plain Sight* exhibit; Boise State symposium

2011
ETA announces "definitive cessation of armed activity"

2014
Anduiza Fronton 100th Anniversary

EGUNGOAK

2014
Boise Basque Catholics welcome Aita Antton Eigiguren Iraoloa

2015–2016
Jaialdi #7; Boise Basque Soccer Friendly game; *Joan Etorri* Basque Studies Symposium; Ikastola moves; Smithsonian *Folklife Festival* - Capitol Mall

2017
Ahaztu Barik Basque cemetery project Eloise Garmendia Bieter Basque Studies Chair, Iñaki Goirizalaia

2018
Museum staff and Basque Market to Basque Country; Museum website; Boise State Basque student radio show; Basque Mural restoration; increased exhibits at museum

The Basque Museum and Cultural Center restored the Cyrus Jacobs-Uberuaga boardinghouse to period authenticity, including a kitchen, dining area, and boarders' rooms. Photo courtesy Erin Ann Jensen.

LIST OF TERMS

Ama	Mother
Amuma	Grandmother, also Amatxi, Amona
Aita	Father
Aitxitxe	Grandfather, also Aitona
Amerikanuak	First-generation Basque immigrants to America
Argizaiola	The "offering of light," made for the deceased. The wood block was carved, then wax candles roped around it. It was lit in remembrance of the deceased both to protect the soul with light and to remind the living of the light that soul shone while on earth.
Auzoa	Rural Basque community, neighborhood
Auzolan	Shared work of the community
Bai	"Yes" in Euskara (*Ez* is the Euskara word for "no")
Baserri	Rural ancestral Basque farmhouse
Baserritarrak	Basques who resided in the rural, countryside/farm areas of the Basque Country
Basque Provinces (Zazpiak Bat, "Seven Are One")	Bizkaia, Gipuzkoa, Araba (Basque Autonomous Community—Spain) Nafarroa (Autonomous Navarre—Spain) Nafarroa Beherea, Lapurdi, Zuberoa (Department Pyrenees Atlantique—France)
Community	*Oxford Dictionary*: "A group of people living in the same place or having a particular characteristic in common;" and "people [of a district or country] considered collectively, especially in the context of social values and responsibilities." In Basque, *komunitatea*, related to *auzoa*..
Cultural Community	*Library of Congress Folklife Center*: "Living expression of culture in everyday life — anyone's culture — learned and passed on informally from person to person. It must be current . . . though it may have existed over long stretches of time."

LIST OF TERMS

Diaspora	Literally, a "dispersed seed." Dispersed ethnic populations living outside their ancestral and historical homelands from their homeland, often traumatically (due to political, social, economic, religious reasons), and in search of work, trade, colonial ambition.
ETA	"Euskadi Ta Askatasuna," (Basque Homeland and Liberty) the violent Basque separatist group that first formed in 1959 to push for greater independence and the end of oppression, abuse of human rights, and disregard for civil liberties by the regime of General Franco against the Basque people. In 2010, a permanent ceasefire was declared that is still in force, and by 2012, the group negotiated an end to the operations and officially disbanded in 2018.[1]
Egungoak	Third+ generations (grandchildren of the first Amerikanuak generation)
Eguzkilore	Ancient Basques placed these dried sunflowers over home doorways as the first greeting to anyone who entered a Basque home. It was placed to ward off evil, provide strength, and protect families.
Eliza	Church
Etorkizunekoak	Future generations
Etxea	Home/House
Etxekoandre	Woman of the House
Etxekojaun	Man of the House
Euskal Herria	The entire Basque Country, seven provinces between Spain and France
Euskara	Basque language
Euskadi	Three provinces of the Basque Autonomous Community (BAC): Bizkaia, Gipuzkoa, Araba
Euskaldunak	Speakers of Euskara (Basque language)

LIST OF TERMS

Foruak	Ancient Basque foral laws (Spanish fueros)
Fronton	Basque handball court. This is the word in English, in Euskara *Frontoia* or *Pilotalekua*.
Gernika (Bombing)	On April 26, 1937, Gernika's civilians, mostly women and children on market day, were bombed by German and Italian airplanes dropping approximately thirty tons of explosives and incendiary bombs. Fleeing civilians were machine-gunned from the air, with the total number of killed approximately two thousand and another one thousand wounded. Artist Pablo Picasso illustrated the horrors suffered in this act of war in a mural, called "Guernica," that became an international icon of repression, war, and horror. [2]
Gernikako Arbola	The entire town of Gernika was destroyed by the 1937 bombing, except for the church and the parliament building with an oak tree in front of it. The "Oak Tree of Gernika" (*Gernikako Arbola*) has stood ever since as a symbol of Basque freedom and endurance. The Lehendakari (President) takes an oath of office under this tree.[3] Boise has two saplings from the Gernikako Arbola: one on Idaho Statehouse grounds, and the other in front of the Basque Museum's Uberuaga boardinghouse on Grove Street.
Habia	Nest
Hasierrak	"Mystery people" (A term for the Basques)
Herria	Place and People
Hegoalde	The four Spanish Basque provinces: Bizkaia, Gipuzkoa, Araba, Nafarroa
Hilarrieta	Village cemetery in the Old Country
Hilarriak	Gravestones/Markers/Funeral Stelae in the Old Country, often decorated with a lauburu, stars, sun, tools of the trade and name of the house
Ikastola	Basque school (language is primary, often for preschool children)
Ikurriña	Basque flag

LIST OF TERMS

Iparralde	The three French Basque provinces: Nafarroa Beherea, Lapurdi, Zuberoa
Jaialdi	"Big Celebration:" Boise's international Basque festival that is held every five years. The next Jaialdi will be in 2020.
Jarleku	The sepulterie/sepulchre seat in the church was once a burial area and the seat of the *etxekoandre*, the woman of the house. This funeral bench was used for funeral offerings.
Jota	A traditional Basque dance
Kaletarrak	Basques who resided in the urban, city areas of the Basque Country
Kalimotxo	American-Basque drink made of Coca-Cola and cheap red wine, over ice
Karro Kampo	Sheepwagon (Basque-American)
Lauburu	Basque symbol (four seasons, cardinal directions, elements of water, earth, water, fire) - literally, "four heads" (*lau* is four; *buru* is head)
Lehendakari	Basque President
Lekuak	Places
Makila	Traditional Basque walking stick that was sometimes also a weapon.
Mari	In Basque mythology, she is the supreme being and most powerful, or mother, of all beings. She lives in the center of the earth, especially connected to caves, and can take many shapes – human, animal, wind, or fire.
Oinkari	"On one's feet," name of Boise's Basque Dancers
Olatak	Funeral food and drink offerings
Omenaldia	Anniversary remembrance ceremony, usually with a Mass celebrated near All Souls' Day to honor the souls of the departed

LIST OF TERMS

Ostatu/Ostatuak	Boardinghouse/Boardinghouses
Pelota/Pilota/Pala	An ancient Basque handball game, played by hitting a hard rubber ball with one's hands against a wall with hands on a 2- or 3-walled court (fronton). It becomes pala if a wooden paddle is used. *Esku* is the hands-only version. Baleen and goma are versions of pala played by women.
Picon Punch	American-made drink with Amer Picon liqueur, sparkling water or ginger ale, float of brandy, maraschino cherry juice, with a lemon twist, on ice. "One is good, two is great, three — you don't remember."
Pintxo	Small appetizer-sized bites of food, shared with others (similar to Spanish tapas)
Tartekoak	Second generation (children of the first Amerikanuak generation)
Transnational	Extending or operating across national boundaries with culture; "here and there": two cultures with dual allegiances; sharing of goods, resources, remittances, money, food, drinks, etc.
Txapela	Basque beret/hat
Zazpiak Bat	"The Seven Are One": Seven Basque provinces often depicted in one coat of arms

Basque food is one highlight of the Basque Block, including croquetas at Bar Gernika. Photo courtesy Meggan Laxalt Mackey.

BOISE: UNIQUELY BASQUE
BOISE'S BASQUE CULTURAL COMPONENTS

Basque cultural persistence is clearly observable in this city. Almost all of these items required auzolan, and they each represent ethnic expression throughout the generations, from Amerikanuak to Tartekoak to Egungoak. Here is a list of Boise's Basque cultural components as of 2017.

A large concentrated Basque population that have remained in the city for over a hundred years
- Boise, Idaho

The only cultural district in the United States
- The Basque Block, between 6th and Capitol Blvd., Boise

The oldest standing indoor public fronton in the United States, still in use
- Anduiza Fronton, built 1914

The only museum-cultural center in the United States (Euskara classes, music and document archives, oral history, artifact, and photo collections, museum exhibits, on-site and off-site educational programs, gift shop, special events)
- Basque Museum and Cultural Center

The only restored Basque boardinghouse in the United States
- Cyrus Jacobs-Uberuaga Boardinghouse (operated by the Basque Museum and Cultural Center)

The first Basque dance group to perform internationally
- Oinkari Basque Dancers

The first University Basque Studies Abroad program
- Boise-Oñati, 1974, Boise State University

The only Ikastola in the United States (State Board of Education-approved)
- Boiseko Ikastola

The first Basque Mayor
- David Bieter, Boise

The first Basque Idaho Secretary of State and successor Secretary of State
- Pete Cenarrusa, followed by Ben Ysursa

The first interpretive exhibit about Basque immigration that traveled to Ellis Island
- "Hidden in Plain Sight," by the Basque Museum and Cultural Center and Boise State University

The first public Basque mural in the United States
- Basque Mural on Capitol Blvd., by the "Letterheads"

Largest area (city district) of Basque cultural interpretation in the United States
- Basque Block, Boise, Idaho (interpretive educational signs, Basque surnames, song lyrics, coats of arms, public art, museum exhibits, events and programs)

The second social center to be built in the United States for the Basques, but first in the West
- The Basque Center, owned and operated by Euzkaldunak, Inc.

The only international Basque cultural festival; held every five years
- Jaialdi, in Boise

A large number of historic boardinghouses during an extended period of time (see Basque boardinghouse map and key, about 52 total through the years); six structures that remain today; multi-state Community History research effort to collect information about several generations of Basques in the American West (led by the Basque Museum and Cultural Center)
- Boise, Idaho

Basque education: formal academic programs, student training, and community education
- Boise State University: Basque Studies (undergraduate studies, minor program, language classes, Basque workshops, cultural symposia and conferences, exchange students)
- Basque Global Collaborative and *BOGA* Basque Studies academic journal
- Cadre of Basque faculty - accredited college courses, workshops, Osher courses
- The first university Basque Studies Chair in honor of a woman - the Eloise Garmendia Bieter Chair at Boise State University, Basque Studies
- Basque Museum educational programs, Euskara classes, on-site library and archives
- Extensive oral history collections and oral history/document/photo collecting from Basques
- Basque Student Club at Boise State University
- Basque Student radio show at Boise State University
- Internship program (Basque Museum, University of Idaho, Boise State University, Ikastola)
- Cenarrusa Foundation for Basque Culture
- Basque Country exchanges and support: Basque Autonomous Community government, University of the Basque Country (EHU), Etxepare Institute
- Collaborative education: University of Nevada, Reno, Boise State University, other universities

An oak sapling planted from the Tree of Gernika
- Oak tree in front of the Cyrus Jacobs- Uberuaga Boardinghouse
- A second sapling from the Gernika tree is planted at the Idaho Statehouse
- A third tree, a sapling from Boise, at Capitol Mall (planted 2016 at Smithsonian Folklife Festival)

A one-time Basque church, with a Basque priest assigned to administer to the Basque congregation
- Church of the Good Shepherd, Father Bernardo Arregui
- 2015: Basque priest from the Basque Country, Father (Aita) Annton Eigiguren

UNIQUELY BOISE

The first multi-state community history project that tells the story of hundreds of Basque families in the American West through videotaped interviews, and in-home scans of photographs and documents. Online access to oral histories, documents, photos. Led by the Basque Museum and Cultural Center.
- *Dorothy Bicandi Aldecoa Community History Project* (Idaho, Oregon, Wyoming, Nevada, California, Washington)

Some of the largest visitor numbers and memberships served in the United States
- Basque Museum and Cultural Center, Euzkaldunak's Basque Center, Boise Fronton Association

Concentrated area of Basque culinary expertise, public dining, drinks and market
- Restaurants: Bar Gernika, Leku Ona, Epi's fine dining and catering(Meridian), Txikiteo
- Basque Market (specialty food and goods, pintxos, catering, special paella meals, culinary tours)
- Drinks: available at all restaurants, as well as at the Basque Center's public bar
- Oinkari Basque Dancers' Chorizo Booth

Monthly member dinners and special events
- Euzkaldunak's Basque Center

Cultural leaders: a few notable persons and groups (not a compete list - historic/contemporary)
- Basque Language/Euskara - Joe Eiguren
- Basque radio show - Espe Alegria
- Basque dance "Mother" - Juanita Uberuaga Hormaechea
- Basque music pioneers - Jimmy Jausoro and Domingo Ansotegui
- Basque bands and music groups - *Txantxangorriak, Amuma Says No*, accordion players
- Biotzetik Basque Choir
- Oinkari Basque Dancers and Onate liturgical dancers

Basque mutual aid societies, associations, cultural organizations (historic/contemporary)
- Basque Girl's Club
- La Sociedad de Socorros Mutuos
- La Fraternidad Vasca Americana
- Aiztan Artean
- Anaiak Danok
- Boiseko Kluba

One of the largest Basque cemetery sections in the United States
- Morris Hill Cemetery, St. John's Catholic Section
- *Unmarked Graves Projects* (including public memorial stone and 59 headstones)

MAPS

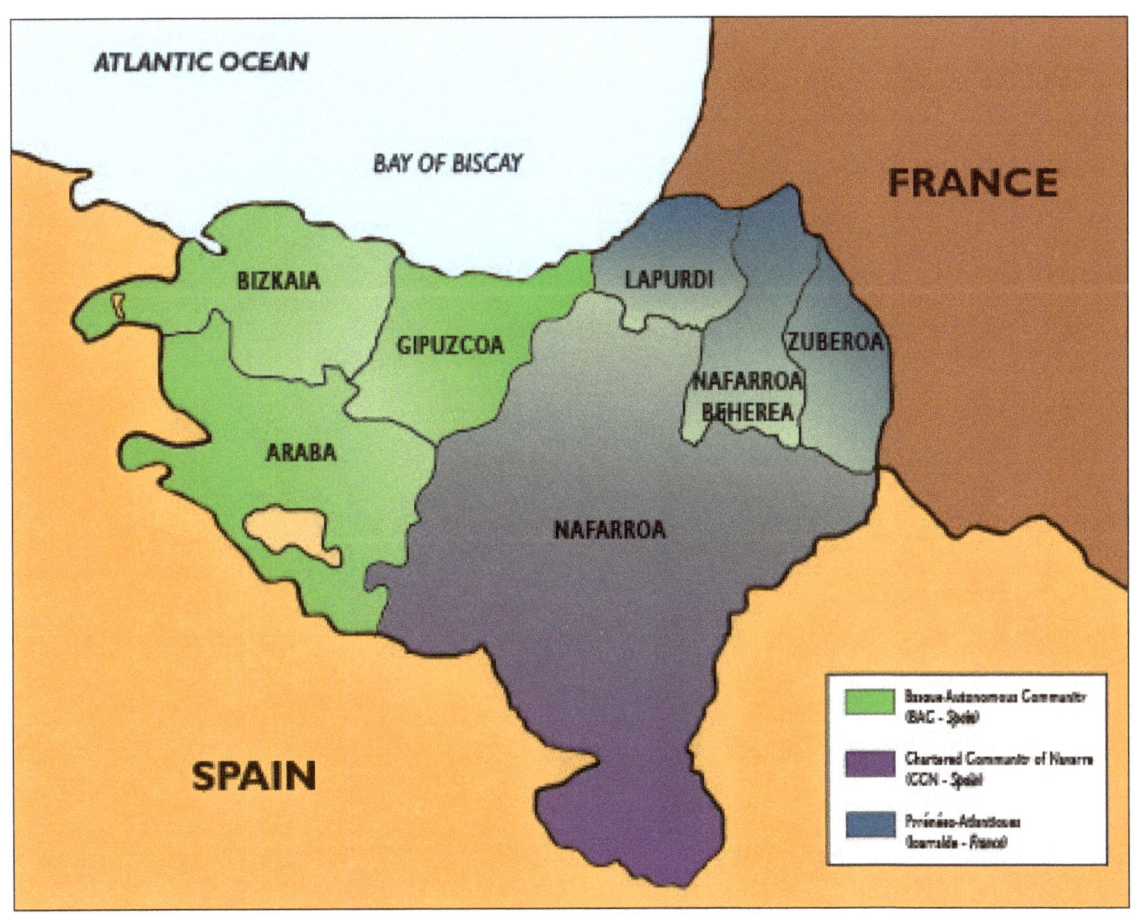

Map of the Basque Country (Euskal Herria). Map courtesy Meggan Laxalt Mackey.

MAPS

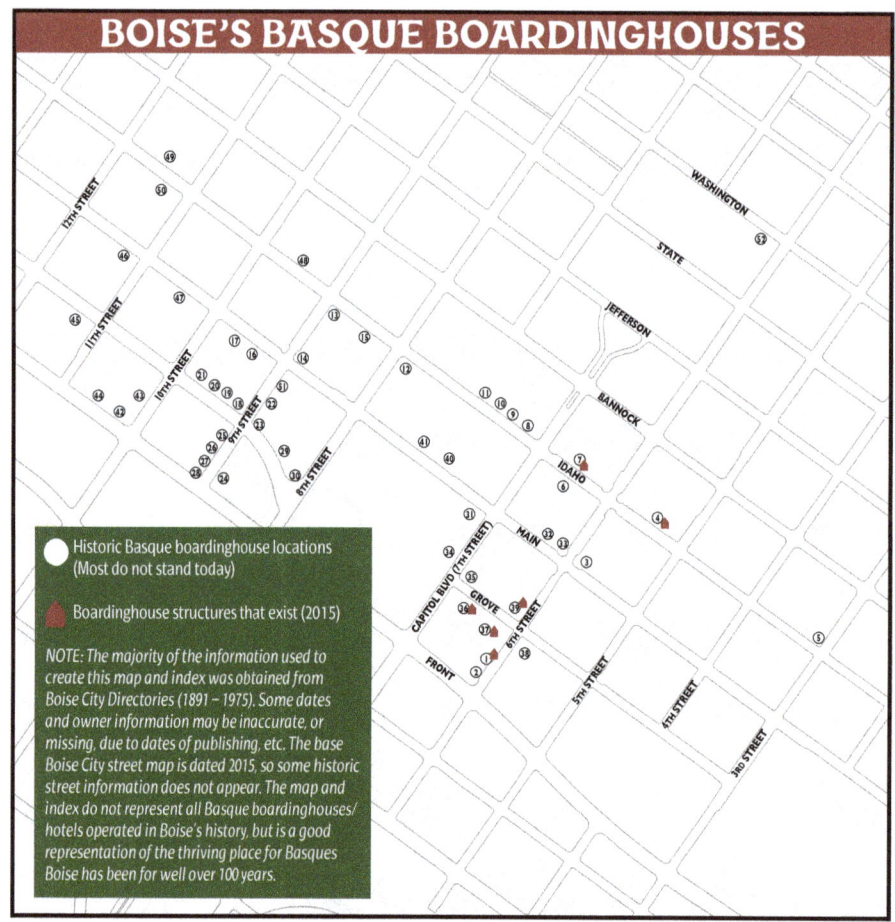

Beginning in the late nineteenth century, the transition to American life for Basque immigrants was eased by Basque-operated boardinghouses, called ostatuak. As early as 1891, Basque boardinghouses in Boise served as "home away from home" for Basque sheepherders in need of lodging, meals, and business or medical assistance when in town. They were also social gathering places that offered the companionship and support of their countrymen, especially in their native Basque language. Boardinghouses played a profound role in preserving Basque culture, including language, food, music, dance, and recreation.

Patty Miller, Basque Museum & Cultural Center

MAPS

OSTATUAK: BOISE'S BASQUE BOARDINGHOUSES

#	Name - Address	Proprietor	Years
46	Ada Hotel - 1009 1/2 Main	Pete & Lottie Echevarria	1950
46	Ada Hotel - 1009 1/2 Main	Mrs. Juanita Arambarri	1956
48	Aguirre, F. - 918 W. Idaho	F. Aguirre	1911-1915
41	Akin Rooms - 724 1/2 Main	Stephen Echevarria	1925
44	Aldape's - 1024 Front with Bolatoki	Felipe Aldape	1912-1914
🏠 24	Anduiza Hotel - 216 S. 9th	Juan C. Anduiza	1912-1914
36	Anduiza Hotel - 619 Grove and Fronton	Juan C. Anduiza	1914-1945
26	Arego/Arguinchona's - 217 1/2 S. 9th	Arego/ Arguinchona	1917-1923
27	Arego's - 217 S. 9th	Benito Arego	1920-1925
28	Arego's Hotel - 219 S. 9th	Benito Arego	1909-1915
48	Arego's Hotel - 918 W. Idaho	Benito Arego	1906-1907
17	Arguinchona's - 915 1/2 Main	Hilario & Laura Arguinchona	1941
🏠 1	Arriola's - 211 S. 6th	Juana Arriola	1917-1921
20	Arrow Rock Hotel - 910 1/2 Grove	Irinio Arredondo	1923
32	Batis' - 612 1/2 Main	Gloria Batis	1937-1948
🏠 39	Belaustegui's - 117 S. 6th	Francisca "Patxa" Belaustegui	1934-1957
34	Belaustegui's - 117 S. 7th	Augustin & Francisca Belaustegui	1918-1934
18	Belaustegui's - 903 Grove	Augustin & Francisca Belaustegui	1911
3	Beverly Rooms - 104 N. 6th	Juana Odiaga	1932-1936
3	Beverly Rooms - 104 N. 6th	Ana Odiaga	1936-1941
32	Bilbao's - 612 1/2 Main	Carmen Bilbao	1938-39
21	Blue Bird Hotel - 912 Grove	Elias Echevarria	1934-1949
21	Blue Bird Hotel - 912 Grove	John & Miren Garechana	1950-1969
15	Boise City Hotel - 811 1/2 W. Idaho	Fructosa Orbea	1930
40	Boise Hotel - 716 1/2 Main	Fructosa Orbea	1929
9	José Uberuaga Lodgings - 706 1/2 Idaho	Jose Uberuaga	1904
9	Capitol Rooms - 706 1/2 W. Idaho	Joe & Crusa Arostegui and Pedro & Maria Epeldi	1912-1942
9	Capitol Rooming Rooms	Crusa Arostegui	1942-1965
14	City Lodging House - 116 N 9th	Jose Uberuaga	1901-1902
14	City Lodging House - 116 N. 9th	J.C. Anduiza	1906-1911
28	Cris' Hotel & Café - 219 S. 9th	Cristobal Sagasti	1956-1961
19	Del Rio - Sabala's - 910 Grove	Paul & Maria Sabala	1953-1974
47	Del Rio Hotel - 1106 1/2 Main	Marie & Paul Sabala	1948
40	Del Rio Hotel - 716 1/2 Main	Marie Sabala	1936-1945
30	Delamar Hotel - 807 Grove	Antonio Letemendi	1912
30	Delamar Hotel - 807 Grove	Vicente Bilbao	1915
30	Delamar Hotel - 807 Grove	Mateo & Adriana Arregui	1920-1925
30	Delamar Hotel - 807 Grove	Mateo Arregui	1925-1928
30	Delamar Hotel - 807 Grove	Mateo & Maria Dominga Arregui	1928-1941
30	Delamar Hotel - 807 Grove	John & Marie Arregui	1941-1945
30	Delamar Hotel - 807 Grove	Hilario & Laura Arguinchona	1945-1969
19	Eagle Hotel - 910 Grove	Felipe Aldape	1929 - 1931
19	Eagle Hotel - 910 Grove	Hilario & Petra Urresti	1932-1947
19	Eagle Hotel - 910 Grove	Juanita Gavica	1948-1950
15	Economy Rooms - 811 1/2 W. Idaho	Justo & Angeles Murelaga	1936-1940
15	Economy Rooms - 811 1/2 W. Idaho	John & Florence Uribe	1941-1943
31	Empress Hotel - 701 1/2 Main	Juan Legarreta	1927
31	Empress Hotel - 701 1/2 Main	John Bastida	1929-1935
31	Empress Rooms - 701 1/2 Main	Laura Arguinchona	1936
40	Etcharte's - 716 1/2 Main	David Etcharte	1923
42	Gabiola's - 1016 Front	Juan Gabiola	1911
49	Goicoechea's - 1116 W. Idaho	Leuterio Goicoechea	1909-1910
51	Hotel Central - 121 1/2 S. 9th Central Hotel	Anthony Padua & Victor Padua	1927-1945
25	Hotel Iberia - 213 S. 9th St. (later Oregon Hotel) & Fronton	Antonio & Agustin Azcuenaga and José Navarro	1911
5	Iberia Hotel - 320 W. Idaho	Azcuenaga and Navarro	1912-1913
50	Jayo's - 1103 W. Idaho	Anastacio Anunci (Amias) Jayo	1912-1915
45	Jayo's - 1107 Grove	Anastacio Jayo	1922-1927
13	José Uberuaga Lodgings - 930 N. 9th	Yturraspe & Jose Uberuaga	1894 - 1899
49	Letemendi's - 1116 W. Idaho	Antonio Letemendi	1915
24	Letemendi's - 216 S. 9th	Antonio & Leandra Letemendi	1918-1927
38	Letemendi's - 521 Grove	Antonio & Leandra Letemendi	1929-1967
10	Lodgings - Gestal - 708-712 Idaho	Joe & Narcisa Gestal	1899
33	Madarieta's - 606 1/2 Main	Isidora Madarieta	1923-1967
31	Majestic Hotel - 701 1/2 Main	Joe Artolazabal	1953
31	Majestic Hotel - 701 1/2 Main	Sally Onaindia	1955
31	Majestic Hotel - 701 1/2 Main	Billie Chacartegui	1958
31	Majestic Hotel - 701 1/2 Main	Ysidor & Polly Aguirre	1961
31	Majestic Hotel - 701 1/2 Main	Frank & Maria Araquistain	1964
31	Majestic Hotel - 701 1/2 Main	Basilio Yzaguirre	1967
23	Metropole - 118 1/2 S. 9th	Victor Gavica	1925
43	Mitchell Hotel - 235 S. 10th	Felipe Aldape	
6	Modern Lodging - 613 (613 1/2) W. Idaho	Mateo & Adriana Arregui	1906-1918
6	Modern Rooming House - 613 (613 1/2) W. Idaho	Eustacio Ormaechea	1918-1927
6	Modern Rooming House - 613 W. Idaho	Benito & Tomas Ysursa	1927-1939
32	Olorriaga's - 612 1/2 Main	Dora Olorriaga	1932-1935
29	Oregon Rooming House - 816 Grove	Anastacio & Anunci Jayo	1918-1925
16	Pacific Hotel - 909 1/2 Idaho	Luis Madarieta	1955
16	Palace Hotel - 909 1/2 Main	Clem & Angeles Areitio	1939
16	Palace Hotel - 909 1/2 Main	Luis Madarieta	1953
22	Royal Hotel - 118 S. 9th	Anastacio & Anunci Jayo	1929-1939
32	Royal Hotel - 612 1/2 Main	Anunci Jayo	1941-1947
32	Royal Hotel - 612 1/2 Main	Frank Goitia	1948-1969
32	Sabala's - 612 1/2 Main	Paul & Maria Sabala	1929
52	Sabala's - 617 W. Washington	Hipolito & Maria Sabala	1920-1930
1	Saracondi's - 211 S. 6th	Juan & Juana Arriola Uberuaga	1909, 1918-21
46	Savory (Savoy) Hotel - 1009 1/2 Main	Boney Bermensolo	1932
8	Spanish Lodging House - 706 Idaho	I.W. Pfost	1901-1903
12	Spanish Restaurant - 8th & Idaho	José & Narcisa Gestal	1891
11	Spanish Restaurant - 712 Idaho	José & Narcisa Gestal	1895
🏠 4	Star Lodging House - 512 W. Idaho and Fronton	Joseph Uberuaga	1906-1913
4	Star Rooming House - 512 W. Idaho	Frank & Gabina Aguirre	c.1915-1974
28	Star Rooms - 219 S. 9th		1929
🏠 37	Uberuaga's - 607 Grove Street with Bolatoki	Jose & Hermenegilda Uberuaga	1917-1967
2	Unamuno - 211 1/2 S. 6th	Unamuno's	1908
🏠 7	Valencia Hotel - Ysursa's - 620 (612) Idaho	Tomas & Benito Ysursa	1941-1969
7	Valencia Hotel - Ysursa's - 620 (612) Idaho	Ramon, Mgr (1958)	1969-1972
		Emeterio Ysursa, Mgr	1969-1972
35	Yribar's, Ybars - 118 S. 7th (later, Capitol Blvd)	John Yribar	1904-1935

The 🏠 house symbol indicates boardinghouse structures that still stand in Boise as of 2018. Boise's Basque ostatuak research conducted by the Basque Museum and Cultural Center Community History Team: Patty Miller, Toni Berria, and Connie Urresti, with support from John Urresti and Celeste Landa, research volunteers, museum curatorial staff, and a host of student interns.

MAPS

MORRIS HILL CEMETERY, ST. JOHN'S SECTION: 1935

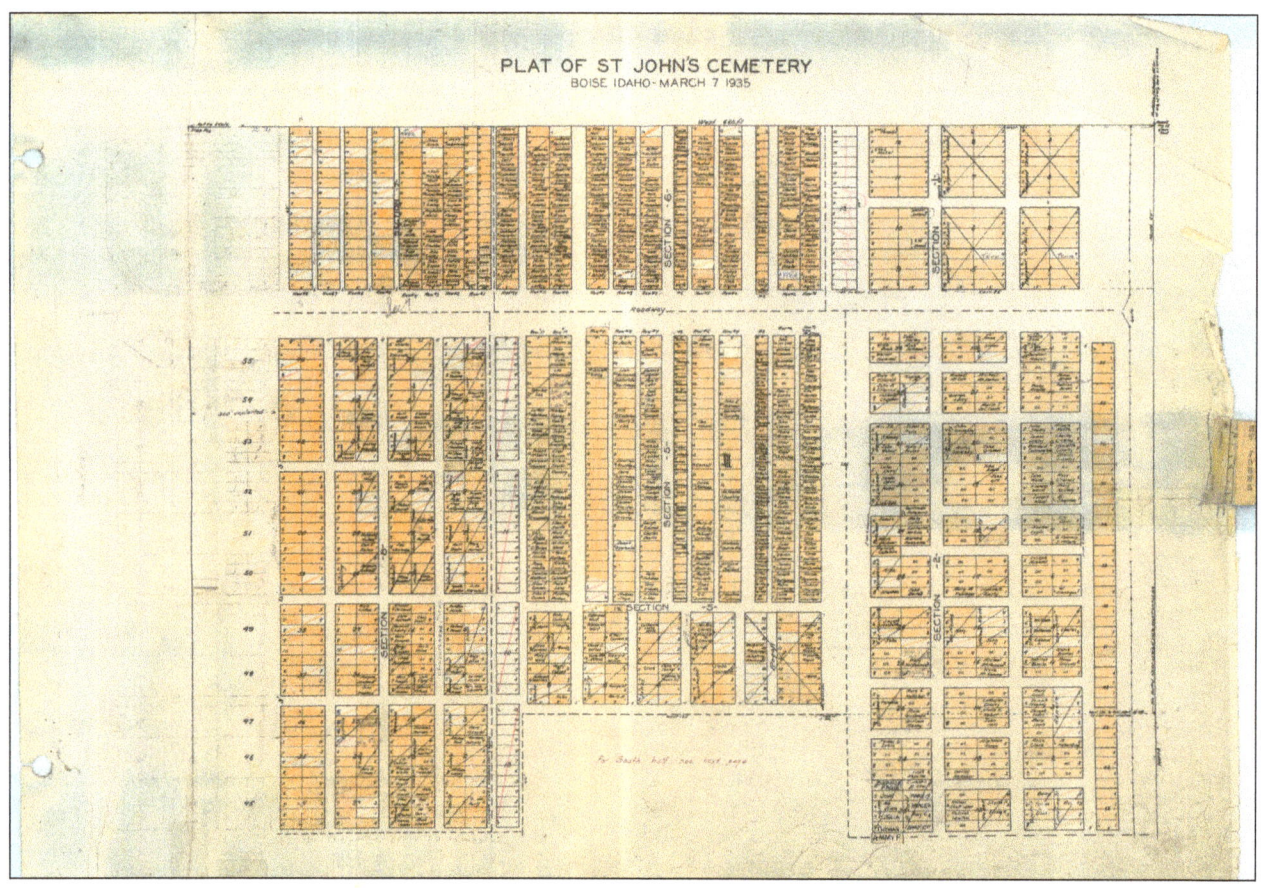

Plot map courtesy City of Boise, Parks and Recreation, Morris Hill Cemetery.

MAPS

MORRIS HILL CEMETERY, ST. JOHN'S SECTION: 1950

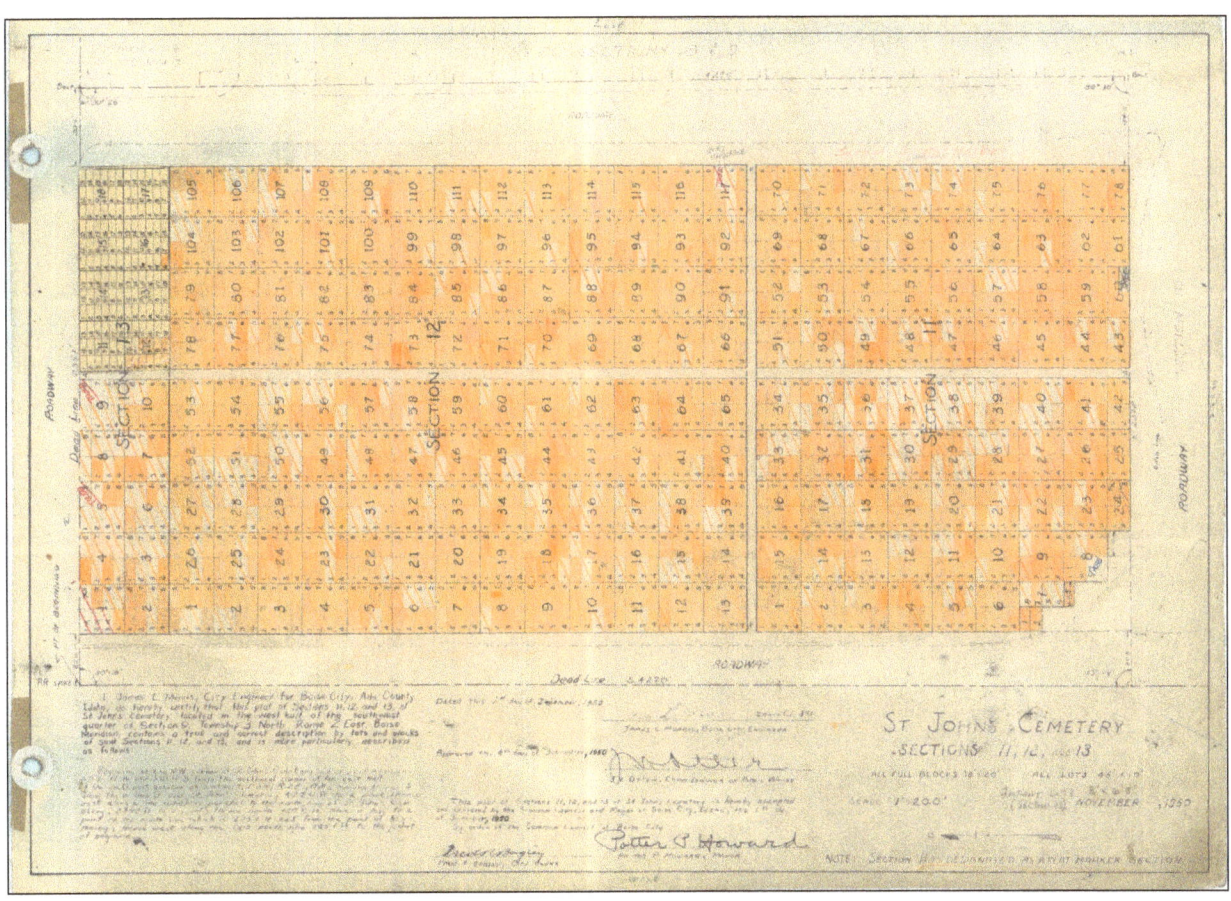

Plot map courtesy City of Boise, Parks and Recreation, Morris Hill Cemetery.

Basque Block construction, May 2000. Photo courtesy
Basque Museum and Cultural Center, Boise, Idaho.

NOTES

PREFACE

1. Gabriel Aresti, *Harri eta Herri (Stone and Country)*. In *The Basque Country: A Cultural History* (Oxford: Oxford University Press, 2008), xxi. *Nire Aitaren Etxea, The House of My Father*, is included in Aresti's poetry collection, *Harri eta Herri*. Woodworth contends that Aresti's *Harri eta Herri* is the most influential collection of poetry published in the last century.

2. John Bieter and Mark Bieter, *An Enduring Legacy: The Story of Basques in Idaho* (Reno: University of Nevada Press, 2000), 17.

3. Etibaliz Amorrortu, *Basque Sociolinguistics: Language, Society, and Culture* (Reno: University of Nevada Reno, Center for Basque Studies, Basque Textbook Series, 2003), 11–17. Note: the subject of Basque language has been widely studied. There are many excellent sources regarding Euskara, its uniqueness, dialects, use throughout history, and foundation for Basque identity. See also R.L. Trask, *History of the Basque* (New York/London: Routledge, 1996; R. L. Trask, *Etymological Dictionary of Basque*, edited for web publication by Max W. Wheeler (Sussex: University of Sussex, 2008 © the estate of the late R. L. Trask); José Hualde, Joseba A. Lakarra, and R.L. Trask, eds., *Towards a History of the Basque Language* (Amsterdam/Philadelphia: John Benjamins Publishing, Volume 131, 1995); José Ignacio Hualde and Koldo Zuazo, "The standardization of the Basque language," *Language Problems and Language Planning* 31.2 (2007): 143–168; Begoña Echeverria, "For whom does language death toll? Cautionary tales from the Basque case," *Linguistics and Education* 21 (2010) 197–209; Gianfranco Forni, "Evidence for Basque as an Indo-European Language," *Journal of Indo-European Studies*, Vol 41, Number 1 and 3, Spring/Summer 2013.

4. Amorrortu, *Basque Sociolinguistics*, Preface.

5. Juan Carlos Etxegoien "Xamar," *Orhipean: The Country of Basque* (Pamplona-Iruña: Udalbide, 2001), 13–15.

6. North American Basque Organizations (NABO), Explanation of zazpiak bat (seven are one) and zortizuak bat (eight are one that includes diaspora) http://www.nabasque.org/old_nabo/NABO/zortziak_Bat.htm.

7. Eusko Jaurlaritzaren/Basque Autonomous Government publication, "Basque Country: Insight into Its Culture, History, Society, and Institutions," available at Boise State University, Basque Studies Program, http://basquestudies.boisestate.edu/wp-content/uploads/2012/09/The-Basque-Country.pdf.

8. William A. Douglass and Jon Bilbao, *Amerikanuak: Basques in The New World* (Reno: University of Nevada Press, 1975), 61–115.

9. Douglass and Bilbao, *Amerikanuak*, 51–60; "Newfoundland and Labrador Heritage Organization," North American Basque Organizations (NABO), http://www.nabasque.org/old_nabo/Pages/arrantzan.htm; "Basque Whaling in Red Bay and Labrador," http://www.heritage.nf.ca/articles/exploration/basque-whaling-red-bay.php; North Atlantic Whale Consortium, http://www.narwc.org/index.php?mc=6&p=10.

10. Gloria Totoricaguena, *Boise Basques: Dreamers and Doers* (Vitoria-Gasteiz: Central Publications Service of the Basque Government, Urazandi Collection, 2002), 25–27.

11. Mark Kurlansky, *The Basque History of the World* (New York: The Penguin Group, 1999), 3.

12. Douglass and Bilbao, *Amerikanuak*, 403.

13. Ibid., 400.

14. Gloria Totoricaguena, *Basque Migration and Diaspora Transnational Identity* (Reno, Nevada: Center for Basque Studies, University of Nevada, Reno, 2005), 48.

15. Totoricaguena, *Basque Migration*, 10.

NOTES

16. Bieter and Bieter, *An Enduring Legacy*, 34; St. John's Parish records, Boise, Idaho, 1863–1952; Oral histories and other documents at the Basque Museum and Cultural Center from first- and second-generation Basques in Boise.
17. Bieter and Bieter, *An Enduring Legacy*, 34.
18. Jeronima Echeverria, *Home Away from Home: A History of Basque Boarding Houses* (Reno: University of Nevada Press, 1999). Echeverria is generally credited with coining the phrase "home away from home" for the Basque boardinghouse in America.
19. Bieter and Bieter, *An Enduring Legacy*, 34.
20. Ibid., 49.
21. Jeronima Echeverria, "Lyda Esain: A Hotelera's Story," in Richard Etulain, ed. *Portraits of Basques in the New World* (Reno: University of Nevada Press, Basque Series, 1999), 155–171.
22. KBOI Boise Radio, "Boise Known for Greatest Concentration of Basques," interview with John Bieter, July 2015, http://www.kboi2.com/news/local/boise_basques-320333341.html

INTRODUCTION

1. William A. Douglass and Joseba Zulaika, "Auzolan," in *Basque Culture: Anthropological Perspectives*. (Reno: University of Nevada, Center for Basque Studies, 2007), Chapter 14, 224–227.
2. Ibid.
3. Ibid.
4. Bieter and Bieter, *An Enduring Legacy*.
5. Carmelo Urza, "The Age of Institutions: Basques in the United States," in *Community in the American West*, ed. Stephen Tchudi (Reno and Las Vegas: Nevada Humanities Committee, 1999), 231–251.
6. William A. Douglass, "Interstitial Culture, Virtual Ethnicity and Hyphenated Basque Identity in the New Millenium," in *Global Vasconia: Essays on the Basque Diaspora* (Reno: University of Nevada Press, 2000); Essay originally published in *Nevada Historical Quarterly*, 43 (2), 2000, 155–165.

CHAPTER I: AMERIKANUAK

1. Bieter and Bieter, *An Enduring Legacy*, 30.
2. Ibid.
3. Ibid., 35–36.
4. Marie Pierre Arrizabalaga, "A Statistical Study of Basque Immigration into California, Nevada, Idaho and Wyoming: 1900–1910" (Master's thesis: University of Nevada, Reno, September 1986), 34.
5. Arrizabalaga, "A Statistical Study of Basque Immigration," 91.
6. Ibid., 92; Arrizabalaga noted that almost all of the 999 Basques counted were first-generation immigrants, with 871 from the Spanish side and 28 from the French side. Second-generation Basques accounted for 5 French and 90 Spanish immigrants; the rest were not identified by generation in this study.
7. Note: Arrizabalaga's entire study provides rich statistical data regarding immigration of Basques to the American West (1900–1910), especially the four states of California, Nevada Idaho, and Wyoming. An interesting source of information, besides U.S. Census and state, city, and county records, are church records. Catholic Church

NOTES

death records at St. John's Parish illustrate the diversity of ethnic groups in Boise, in particular; See also Todd Shallat, *Ethnic Landmarks: Ten Historic Places that Define the City of Trees - Boise City Walking Series* (Boise: Boise City Office of the Historian, Boise State University School of Social Sciences and Public Affairs, 2007), multiple sections of the book.

8. Stephen Tchudi, ed. *Community in the American West* (Reno and Las Vegas: Nevada Humanities Committee, 1999), xiii.

9. Todd Shallat, *Ethnic Landmarks: Ten Historic Places that Define the City of Trees* (Boise: Boise City Office of the Historian, Boise State University School of Social Sciences and Public Affairs, 2007), Boise City Walking Series - multiple sections of the book.

10. Paddy Woodworth, "Foreword," in *Gardeners of Identity: Basques in the San Francisco Bay Area*, ed. Pedro Oiarzabal (Reno: University of Nevada, Center for Basque Studies, Basque Diaspora and Migration Series, no. 4, 2009), 23.

11. Jean S. Phinney, "A Three-Stage Model of Ethnic Identity Development in Adolescence" in *Ethnic Identity: Formation and Transmission among Hispanics and Other Minorities*, Martha E. Bernal and George P. Knight, (Albany: State University of New York Press, 1993), 68–71. Phinney, "A Three-Stage Model of Ethnic Identity Development," 68.

12. Etxegoien "Xamar," *Orhipean*, 28–31.

13. Douglass and Zulaika,"Auzolan," 224–227.

14. Jeronima Echeverria, "Home Away From Home," in *Etxea: The Cyrus Jacobs-Uberuaga House* (Boise: Basque Museum & Cultural Center, 2010), 91–96; and Echeverria, *Home Away From Home*, 7–11.

15. Ibid.

16. Ibid.

17. Basque Museum & Cultural Center, "Ostatuak: A Basque Sense of Home" boardinghouse display, Boise exhibit panels (Boise, 2015); Refer to Boise Basque boardinghouse map in Appendix.

18. Angeles Aldape Murelaga, interview with author, 2007; and Basque Museum and Cultural Center, Angeles Aldape Murelaga oral history.

19. Ibid.

20. Refer to the map of Boise's Basque Boardinghouse in the Appendix. This research was conducted by the Basque Museum and Cultural Center's Dorothy Bicandi Aldecoa Community History project, Patty Miller, Toni Berria, and Connie Urresti, July, 2015; additional related information gathered 2016–2018 by museum curatorial staff and volunteers Dave Lachiondo, Celeste Landa, and John Urresti.

21. Ibid.

22. John Ysursa. "Invisible Cargo," in *Etxea: The Cyrus Jacobs-Uberuaga House*. (Boise: Basque Museum and Cultural Center, 2010), 89–90; See also John and Mark Bieter, "Boise's Wrigley Field," 65–83; and Heidi Coon and John Ysursa, "Work Hard, Play Hard," 85–86, in *Becoming Basque: Ethnic Heritage on Boise's Grove Street* (Boise: Boise State University "Investigate Boise" Community Research Series, Basque Studies program, and the Basque Museum and Cultural Center, 2014).

23. *The Idaho Statesman*, January 29, 1915, in Bieter and Bieter, "Boise's Wrigley Field," *Becoming Basque*, 70.

24. Henry Alegria, *75 Years of Memoirs* (Caldwell: The Caxton Printers, 1981), 139.

NOTES

25. Ibid.

26. Ibid.

27. Pam Demo, "Boise's River Street Neighborhood: Lee, Ash, and Lovers Lane/Pioneer Streets: The South Side of the Tracks" (master's thesis, University of Idaho, April, 2006).

28. William "Bill" White, "The River Street History Project "Day of Archaeology 2015," http://www.riverstreethistory.com/day-of-archaeology-2015-the-river-street-archaeology-project and http://www.riverstreethistory.com/about-the-river-street-digital-history-project.

29. Alegria, *75 Years of Memoirs*, 139–143; Reference from an *Idaho Statesman* story, (exact date unknown) December, 1910.

30. Ibid.

31. Basque Museum and Cultural Center, "Ostatuak: A Sense of Home" boardinghouse exhibit, Boise interpretive exhibit panels, 2015, source: *Idaho Statesman* article, (exact date unknown) December, 1910.

32. Alegria, *75 Years of Memoirs*, 139–143.

33. Basque Museum & Cultural Center, "Ostatuak: A Sense of Home" boardinghouse exhibit, Boise interpretive exhibit panels, 2015, source: *Idaho Statesman* article, September 24, 1914.

34. Bieter and Bieter, *An Enduring Legacy*, 56.

35. Bieter and Bieter, "Wrigley Field," in *Becoming Basque*, 79.

36. Ibid.

37. Totoricaguena, *Boise Basques: Dreamers and Doers* (Vitoria-Gasteiz: Central Publications Service of the Basque Government, Urazandi Collection, 2002), 213.

38. Susan Hardwick, "Russians in the Sacramento Valley," in *Homelands: A Geography of Culture and Place Across America*, ed. Richard L. Nostrand and Lawrence E. Estaville (Baltimore: Johns Hopkins University Press, published with the Center for American Places, Santa Fe, New Mexico and Harrisonburg, Virginia, 2001), 218.

39. Rodney Gallop. *A Book of the Basques* (London: MacMillan Publishing, 1930; Reprinted Reno: University of Nevada Press, 1970), 230.

40. Totoricaguena, *Boise Basques*, 21.

41. Sue Paseman, "The Church of the Good Shepherd," in *Becoming Basque*, 50.

42. St. John's Catholic Parish and Mission records: *Registrum Matrimonium Hispanorum* 1896–1922.

43. Urza, "Age of Institutions," in *Community in the West*, 234.

44. Rt. Rev. Cyprian Bradley, O.S.B., and Most Rev. Edward J. Kelly, D.D., Ph.D., *History of the Diocese of Boise: 1863–1952, Volume 1* (Boise: Roman Catholic Diocese of Boise, 1953 – note: Book cover indicates 1953, title page has 1952), 307.

45. Ibid.

46. Various St. John's Catholic Parish and Mission records contain information about Fr. Arregui's extensive travels for marriages, baptisms, and burials throughout Idaho, Oregon, and Utah between 1911 and 1921.

47. Paseman, *Becoming Basque*, 50–51

48. Bieter and Bieter, *An Enduring Legacy*, 63–64.

49. St. John's Parish and Mission records, *Registrum Matrimonium Hispanorum, 1896–1922*.

50. Ibid.

51. Bieter and Bieter, *An Enduring Legacy*, 64.

NOTES

52. United States State Department, "1921–1936 Immigration Acts; 1917: Asiatic "Barred Zone," Chinese Exclusion Act; Japanese and Filipino Colony," http:history.state.gov/milestones

53. Bieter and Bieter, *An Enduring Legacy*, 62–66; Paseman, "The Church of the Good Shepherd," in *Becoming Basque* and the Basque Museum & Cultural Center, 2014), 49–63; Interpretive sign at the former Church of the Good Shepherd, Idaho Street, Boise, Idaho.

54. Basque Museum and Cultural Center, Interpretive sign at the former Church of the Good Shepherd, Idaho Street, Boise, Idaho.

55. Paseman, in *Becoming Basque*, 56.

56. Bieter and Bieter, *An Enduring Legacy*, 64–65.

57. Bieter and Bieter, *An Enduring Legacy*, 65; See also U.S. Department of State, Office of the Historian. https://history.state.gov/milestones/1921-1936/immigration-act.

58. In 2015, Boise's Basque Catholics have another priest: Father Annton Egiguren Iraola, who was born in the baserri Arretxea in the town of Bidegoian. It is just outside Tolosa, coincidentally, the home village of Father Bernardo Arregui; *Artzai Ona, Boise Basque Catholic Community*, http://basquecatholic.org.

59. Phinney, "A Three-Stage Model of Ethnic Identity Development," 68.

60. Bieter and Bieter, *An Enduring Legacy*, 81–83.

CHAPTER II: TARTEKOAK

1. Bieter and Bieter, *An Enduring Legacy*, 87.

2. Ibid., 95–97.

3. Ibid., 74.

4. Clifford A. Sather, "Marriage Patterns Among the Basques of Shoshone, Idaho," Reed College thesis, 1961), 33, in John Bieter, "Basques, Basque-Americans, American-Basques" (master's thesis, Boise State University, April 1994), 37.

5. *Boise Capital News*, Jun 29, 1937 in Bieter, "Basques, Basque-Americans, American-Basques," 38.

6. William Douglass, "Foreword," in Robert Laxalt, *Sweet Promised Land* (Reno: University of Nevada Press, 1986 – reprint of the 1957 edition, New York: Harper & Row), x.

7. Bieter and Bieter, *An Enduring Legacy*, 155.

8. Teresa Aldape and Angeles Aldape Murelaga, Interview with author, 2006, and family history by author for the Murelaga-Aldape family, *Strength of Family: Felipe and Maria Josefa Aldape*, March 2007.

9. Bieter and Bieter, *An Enduring Legacy*, 69.

10. Laxalt, *Sweet Promised Land*, 134.

11. Douglass, "Foreword," in *Sweet Promised Land*, xiii.

12. Bieter and Bieter, *An Enduring Legacy*, 74; Basque Museum and Cultural Center oral histories. Adelia Garro Simplot, interview conducted by Patty Miller, 12/18/01. http://basquemuseum.com/content/simplot-adelia-garro-0.

13. Author interview with Teresa Aldape and Angeles Aldape Murelaga, 2006; See also *Idaho Food Dealer Magazine*, "Idaho's 1958 Showcase: Corner Grocery of Boise," 1958; The Corner Grocery operated from 1944 to 1969.

14. Patty A. Miller, "They Made This Their Home," in *Etxea: The Cyrus Jacobs-Uberuaga House*, ed. Meggan Laxalt Mackey (Boise: Basque Museum and Cultural Center, 2010), 106–107.

NOTES

15. Patty A. Miller, Basque Museum and Cultural Center, various records and oral histories; See also Bieter and Bieter, *An Enduring Legacy*, 75.
16. Bieter and Bieter, *An Enduring Legacy*, 75.
17. City of Boise, Department of Parks and Recreation, Morris Hill Cemetery, burial records: St. John's Sections 4–13; Cemetery plats.
18. Liz Hardesty's "Unmarked Basque Graves Project," 1996 that was based on church, mortuary, and city cemetery death and burial records; and St. John's Catholic parish death and burial records.
19. Author interview with Liz (Arregui-Dick) Hardesty, July 16, 2015; See also "Don't Let Me Be Forgotten," IGS Quarterly, Autumn 1998; and Gloria Totoricaguena, "Yes, We Remember You," date unknown.
20. Bieter and Bieter, *An Enduring Legacy*, 48; See also Totoricaguena, *Boise Basques*, 222.
21. Bieter and Bieter, *An Enduring Legacy*, 73.
22. Totoricaguena, *Boise Basques*, 91–93.
23. Bieter and Bieter, *An Enduring Legacy*, 99.
24. Basque Museum and Cultural Center, "Ostatuak: A Sense of Home" boardinghouse exhibit, Boise interpretive exhibit panels, 2015.
25. Bieter and Bieter, *An Enduring Legacy*, 100.
26. *Boise Capitol News*, December 19, 1936, in Bieter and Bieter, *An Enduring Legacy*, 100.
27. Gloria Totoricaguena, *Boise Basques*, 234–35; Bieter and Bieter, *An Enduring Legacy*, 100–101.
28. Valencia advertisement, Ysursa family.
29. Bieter and Bieter, *An Enduring Legacy*, 104–107.
30. Totoricaguena, *Boise Basques*, 226; The *2015 Jaialdi Program* lists all of the charter member names.
31. Bieter, "Basques, Basque-Americans, American-Basques," 41.
32. Totoricaguena, *Boise Basques*, 226; See also Christine Hummer, "Basque Center," in *Becoming Basque*, 157–167.
33. Hummer, "Basque Center," in *Becoming Basque*, 158.
34. Membership as of August 31, 2018. Personal communication, Tyler Smith, President of Euzkaldunak, Inc., September 2, 2018. Of note, the Basque Center (Euzkaldunak) membership is restricted to only those of [proven] Basque descent. Personal communication on September 2, 2018 with Annie Gavica, Executive Director of the Basque Museum and Cultural Center's membership is open to all, regardless of ancestry. 2018 membership as of August 31, 2018 was 862 members, which includes "households," family, and corporate members, making the total numbers higher.
35. Bieter, "Basques, Basque-Americans, American-Basques," 44.

CHAPTER III: EGUNGOAK

1. Bieter, "Basques, Basque-Americans, American-Basques." John Bieter first termed these three generations of Basques in the American diaspora in this Master's thesis. See "Basques, Basque-Americans, American-Basques," 57.
2. Jill Gill, Boise State University History Department, personal communication, September 2015.
3. Ibid.
4. Douglass, "Foreword," in *Sweet Promised Land*, xi.

NOTES

5. Ibid.
6. Bieter and Bieter, *An Enduring Legacy*, 121.
7. Iker Saitua,"Sparks Basque Festival - 1959," in *Elko Daily Free Press*, July 17, 2018; accessed August 30, 2018: https://elkodaily.com/lifestyles/basque-festival-the-woodstock-of-the-basque-american-community-in/article_471203c4-c5f5-5d7d-b903-10e5d0bdc176.html.
8. Douglass, *Global Vasconia*, 274.
9. Bieter and Bieter, *An Enduring Legacy*, 115–118.
10. Douglass and Bilbao, *Amerikanuak*, 9; See also Boise State University Basque Studies website, http://basquestudies.boisestate.edu/gutaz-basques/basque-basics.
11. Bieter and Bieter, *An Enduring Legacy*, 122–123; See also Bieter, "Basques, Basque-Americans, American-Basques," 57.
12. Ibid.
13. Bieter and Bieter, *An Enduring Legacy*, 126.
14. Ibid., 127.
15. Phinney, "A Three-Stage Model of Ethnic Identity," 71.
16. Bieter and Bieter, *An Enduring Legacy*, 127.
17. Boise State University, Basque Studies Program, Joan Etorri Symposium, July 2015, Boise: http://basquestudies.boisestate.edu.
18. Urza, "The Age of Institutions," 238.
19. Totoricaguena, *Boise Basques*, 174–180.
20. Ibid.
21. Ibid.
22. Ibid.
23. Ibid, 176.
24. Ibid., 177.
25. Basque Museum and Cultural Center, Mission Statement, https://www.basquemuseum.eus
26. Basque Museum and Cultural Center, "About Us" Website, https://www.basquemuseum.eus
27. Annie Gavica, Executive Director of the Basque Museum and Cultural Center, personal communication, September 2, 2018
28. Bieter and Bieter, *An Enduring Legacy*, 123.
29. Bieter and Bieter, "Wrigley Field" in *Becoming Basque*, 79.
30. Bieter and Bieter, *An Enduring Legacy*, photo caption, pala photograph, courtesy Basque Museum and Cultural Center.
31. Ibid., 123.
32. Totoricaguena, *Boise Basques*, 213–214.
33. Annie Gavica, Basque Museum and Cultural Center and Boise Fronton Association, personal communication, Jerry Aldape, Boise Fronton Association.
34. Totoricaguena, *Boise Basques*, 216–217.
35. Bieter and Bieter, "Wrigley Field," in *Becoming Basque*, 82–83.
36. Bieter and Bieter, *An Enduring Legacy*, 153.

NOTES

37. Dave Lachiondo, personal communication, October 2015.
38. Author interview with Liz (Arregui-Dick) Hardesty, July 16, 2015; See also the *IGS Quarterly*, Autumn 1998, and Gloria Totoricaguena's article "Yes, We Remember You," date unknown, and the Unmarked Graves Project Memorial Program, June 23, 1996.
39. Gloria Totoricaguena, "Yes, We Remember You," date unknown.
40. Author interview with Liz (Arregui-Dick) Hardesty, July 16, 2015.
41. Meggan Laxalt Mackey, "Cultural Landmarks," in *Becoming Basque*, 113–115.
42. Boise State University, Basque Global Collaborative: *Artzainak Gogoan*, John Ysursa and Meggan Laxalt Mackey, 2017.
43. Personal communication with Nerea Lete, co-founder of the Boiseko Ikastola; Also Lete lecture, "To Be or Not To Be: Identity," University Foundations UF100 course, Boise State University, October 2015.
44. Totoricaguena, *Boise Basques*, 106.
45. Author e-mail interview with Nerea Lete, co-founder of the Boiseko Ikastola, and Izaskun Kortazar, Euskara teacher and former teacher at the Boiseko Ikastola, in response to questions about "Ikastola and Cultural Persistence," September 2015.
46. Ibid.
47. Berriochoa, "Saving Euskara," in *Becoming Basque*, 38–47.
48. Ibid.
49. Totoricaguena, *Boise Basques*, 108.
50. Author email interview with Nerea Lete, co-founder of the Boiseko Ikastola, in response to questions about "Ikastola and Cultural Persistence," September 2015.
51. Ibid.
52. *Boiseko Ikastola* website, http://www.boisekoikastola.org/ikastola-history.
53. Meggan Laxalt Mackey, "Cultural Landmarks," in *Becoming Basque*, 113.
54. Bieter and Bieter, *An Enduring Legacy*, 5.
55. Basque Museum and Cultural Center, Mission Statement, http://www.basquemuseum.eus
56. William A. Douglass, "Basques in the American West," in *To Build in a New Land: Ethnic Landscapes in North America*, ed. Allen G. Noble (Baltimore and London: The Johns Hopkins University Press, 1992), 392.

AURRERA

1. Jennifer Shelby, "Remaking Grove," in *Becoming Basque*, 195; The Basque Marketplace group was comprised of an organization represented by Mary Kay Aucutt, Francis "Patxi" Lostra, the Basque Museum and Cultural Center, Euzkaldunak, Inc., and the Oinkari Basque Dancers.
2. Ibid.
3. Ibid.
4. Ibid.
5. Totoricaguena, *Boise Basques*, 195–199.
6. Ibid.
7. Bieter and Bieter, *An Enduring Legacy*, 120; See also Mary Waters' social theory elsewhere in Lekuak.

NOTES

8. Pello Salaburu, *Koldo Mitxelena: Selected Writings of a Basque Scholar* (Reno: University of Nevada Reno, Center for Basque Studies, Basque Classics Series, no. 4, 2008), 47.

9. Meggan Laxalt Mackey, "Cultural Landmarks," in *Becoming Basque*, 99–115.

10. *Caldwell Tribune/Idaho Free Press*, May 21, 1970, in Bieter, "Basques, Basque-Americans, American-Basques," 51.

11. The beginning of the historiography of Basques in the American West is most often credited to the 1957 publication of *Sweet Promised Land* by Robert Laxalt, a story of his immigrant sheepherder father's return to the homeland. This was a story about Basque and American identity, and the cultural forces that surrounded the issues of immigration and assimilation into larger American society for the Amerikanuak and Tartekoak Basques.

12. Bieter and Bieter, *An Enduring Legacy*, 5; and Marcus Lee Hansen, "The Third Generation," in *The Children of the Uprooted* (New York: Braziller, 1966).

13. Ibid., Bieter and Bieter, *An Enduring Legacy*, 158.

14. Tyler Smith, Euzkaldunak President personal communication, September 2, 2018.

15. Annie Gavica, Executive Director of the Basque Museum and Cultural Center, personal communication, September 2, 2018.

16. Douglass, "Interstitial Culture," in *Global Vasconia* originally published in *Nevada Historical Quarterly*, 155–165.

17. Ibid.

18. Ibid.

19. Douglass, "Basques in the American West," in *To Build in a New Land*, 392.

20. Phinney, "A Three-Stage Model of Ethnic Identity Development."

21. Herbert J. Gans, "The coming darkness of late-generation European American ethnicity," in *Ethnic and Racial Studies*, vol. 37, no. 5, June 2014, 758.

22. Waters, *Ethnic Options*, 16 and 89.

23. Mary Waters, "Ethnic identities in the future: the possible effects of mass immigration and genetic testing," in *Ethnic and Racial Studies*, vol. 37, no. 5, 2014, 767.

POSTSCRIPT: WHY BOISE?

1. North American Basque Organizations (NABO), "U.S. Basque Population in 2000," http://www.nabasque.org/us_basque_population.html; http://www.nabasque.org/old_nabo/NABO/zenbat_gara.htm; The estimates were based on self-identification and a sampling of Basque ethnicity; Western state estimates included California, 20,868 Basques; Idaho, 6,637 Basques; Nevada, 6,096 Basques; Washington, 2,665 Basques; Oregon, 2,627 Basques; and Wyoming, 869 Basques. These estimates may an under-representation, as many Basques who did not distinctly self-identify as a separate ethnic group identified themselves as "white" or "caucasian." Also, the 2000 census number was derived from a sampling (John Ysursa, personal communication, November 2015).

2. Nancy Zubiri, *Travel Guide to America: Families, Feasts and Festivals* (Reno: University of Nevada Press, Center for Basque Studies, Basque Diaspora and Migration Series, No. 3, 2006, 2007 2nd ed., 1998), 356–357; In a fourteen-year period this number appears high, but it is also likely that more Basques self-identified, along with a population increase in Boise and a new generation of Basques that could self-identify; U.S. Census data: Boise City,

NOTES

2010–2014, http://quickfacts.census.gov/qfd/states/16/1608830.html; Idaho's total statewide population in this study was estimated at 1,634,464; See also North American Basque Organizations (NABO), "U.S. Basque Population in 2000," http://www.nabasque.org/us_basque_population.html; "Idaho's Ethnic Diversity on the Rise," *Idaho Mountain Express*, July 3, 2015, http://www.mtexpress.com/news/blaine_county/idaho-s-ethnic-diversity-on-the-rise/article_a9b96314-20f0-11e5-bae1-7be298a58a51.html.

3. U.S. Census, http://quickfacts.census.gov/qfd/states/32/3260600.html; North American Basque Organizations (NABO), "U.S. Basque Population in 2000," and "U.S. Basques by City," http://www.nabasque.org/us_basque_population.html.

4. North American Basque Organizations (NABO), "U.S. Basque Population in 2000," and "U.S. Basques by City," http://www.nabasque.org/us_basque_population.html; http://quickfacts.census.gov/qfd/states/32/3284800.html.

5. Preservation Idaho, "Boise Architecture Project," boisearchitecture.org/structuredetail.php?id=1715: The German Turnverein Society meeting hall was built in 1906, but closed by 1916 due to pre-World War I anti-German sentiment; Boise City Department of Arts & History, http://www.boiseartsandhistory.org/media/21688/BoiseChinatownGuide.pdf: Various Chinese sites existed in Boise from 1898 to the 1940s, even under the U.S. Chinese Exclusion Act, but anti-Asian eradication and urban renewal claimed most Chinese sites; Preservation Idaho, "Boise Architecture Project," http://www.boisearchitecture.org/structuredetail.php?id=1417: The Sts. Constantine and Helen Greek Orthodox Church was built in Boise's North end, but later, in 1951. It remains today and is one example of Greek cultural persistence, along with the Jewish Synagogue (Temple Ahavath Beth Israel), that was originally built in 1896 near downtown at Eleventh and State Streets, and was later moved to Latah Street in 2003: Preservation Idaho, "Boise Architecture Project," http://boisearchitecture.org/structuredetail.php?id=108; For further study of other immigrant groups in Boise, see: Todd Shallat, *Ethnic Landmarks: Ten Historic Places that Define the City of Trees - Boise City Walking Series* (Boise: Boise City Office of the Historian, Boise State University School of Social Sciences and Public Affairs, 2007), multiple sections of the book - Chinese: 91–97; German, 75–81; Greeks, 123–129.

6. River Street Digital History Project: http://www.riverstreethistory.com/; Idaho Black History Museum, http://www.ibhm.org/; See earlier references to Pam Demo, "Boise's River Street Neighborhood," Master's thesis, April 2006.

7. U.S. Census data: Boise City, 2010–2014, http://quickfacts.census.gov/qfd/states/16/1608830.html; Solely-white population of Boise was 89%; Hispanics/Latinos 7.1%; Asians at 3.2%.

8. David H. Bieter, Mayor of Boise, Speech delivered July 28, 2005 at Jaialdi opening ceremony, "Gernika, Gure Ahizpa - A Celebration of Boise's Basque Sister City," http://mayor.cityofboise.org/speeches/archivedspeeches/2005/07/gernika,-gure-ahizpa-a-celebration-of-boise's-basque-sister-city.

9. Jennifer Shelby, in *Becoming Basque*, 195; The city and county have supported the Basque Block since its creation in 2000 with economic support through grants, public programs, street development, property maintenance, and other civic benefits. Just to establish the Block, the City dedicated $100,000; Boise City's Visual Arts Advisory Committee appropriated $28,000; Capitol City Development Corporation (CCDC) revamped Grove Street at a cost of $100,000; and Ada County Highway District (ACHD) contributed $50,000; See also Totoricaguena, *Boise Basques*, 195–199.

NOTES

10. Annie Gavica, Basque Museum & Cultural Center, personal communication, November 30, 2015.
11. EuskalKazeta Basque News, accessed 09/06/18, www.euskalkazeta.com
12. Marty Peterson, City Club of Boise, July 22, 2015, To hear the program "Boise's Basque Community: A Continuing History," by Drs. John Bieter and John Ysursa, go to http://www.cityclubofboise.org/events/forum-boises-basque-community-a-continuing-history.
13. KTVB television, "Athletic Bilbao defeats Club Tijuana in historic event," July 18, 2015, http://www.ktvb.com/story/sports/2015/07/18/basque-soccer-friendly-recap/30371835; the official count for the historic first-time Basque soccer event in Boise was 21,948 attendees in Boise State University's Albertsons Stadium. Another first with this event: the blue turf was replaced with live green grass.
14. Shallat, *Ethnic Landmarks*, "Chinese," 91–97.
15. Pam Demo, Master's Thesis, 2006.
16. U.S. Census, Business Quick Facts, http://quickfacts.census.gov/qfd/states/16000.html.
17. Bieter and Bieter, *An Enduring Legacy*, 39.
18. Gloria Totoricaguena, *Basque Diaspora*, "Homeland-Diaspora Relations," 528–541.
19. Basque Museum and Cultural Center, "Basque Autonomous Government fiscal contributions recap 1996–2014," November, 2015.
20. Lehendakari Iñigo Urkullu Renteria, (Basque President), "Jaialdi 2015," *The Spokesman Review*, July 29, 2015; accessed August 30 2018.

LIST OF TERMS

1. Author e-mail interview with Dave Lachiondo, "Basque Politics," September 2015.
2. Ibid. See also: Comprehensive writing about the bombing of Gernika and Basque genocide studies has been done by Xabier Irujo: *The Bombing of Gernika: A Short History*, and *Gernika 1937: The Market Day Massacre*.
3. Bieter and Bieter, *Enduring Legacy*, 20.

BOISE: UNIQUELY BASQUE

1. This Basque Boise list was compiled from various sources, including Basque Studies class lectures at Boise State University (Dr. John Bieter, Dr. John Ysursa, Dr. David Lachiondo, Argia Beristain Dougherty, Izaskun Kortazar, and Xabier Irujo); Basque Museum and Cultural Center records; Boiseko Ikastola records; St. John's Parish and the Boise Catholic Diocese church records; Boise City Parks and Recreation cemetery records; Euzkaldunak Basque Center records; Boise'ko Fronton Association records; Boise State University's Basque Studies "Joan Etorri" Basque Symposium, 2015; Bieter, Shallat, et. al, *Becoming Basque*; Bieter and Bieter, *An Enduring Legacy*; Oinkari Basque Dancers; various Jaialdi programs; local newspapers, archival infomration from the University of Nevada, Reno, and a host of documented sources and anecdotal stories. (See *Lekuak* Endnotes and Bibliography.)

Basque sheepherder in Idaho, c. 1925-1928. Photo by "Boise by Burns," courtesy Basque Museum and Cultural Center, Boise, Idaho.

BIBLIOGRAPHY

Aguirre, Iñaki Arizmendi. "General Secretary of Foreign Action for the Basque Government in Euzkadi's Message." In *Boise Basques: Dreamers and Doers*. Reno: University of Nevada, Center for Basque Studies, 2004.

Aguirre, José Antonio. *Escape Via Berlin: Eluding Franco in Hitler's Europe*. Reno: University of Nevada Press. Originally written 1944; English edition 1991.

Alba, Richard. *Italian Americans: Into the Twilight of Ethnicity*. Englewood Cliffs: Prentice-Hall, Inc., 1985.

———. "The twilight of ethnicity: what relevance for today?" Ethnic and Racial Studies 37, no. 5 (2014): 780–85.

Alegria, Henry. *75 Years of Memoirs*. Caldwell: The Caxton Printers, Ltd., 1981.

Allard, William A., and Robert Laxalt. *A Time We Knew: Images of Yesterday in the Basque Homeland*. Reno: University of Nevada Press, 1990.

Alzola, Arsen. *The Basque Experience from the Pyrenees to the Owyhees*. Murphy: Owyhee County Historic Society, 1992.

Amorrortu, Estibaliz. *Basque Sociolinguistics: Language, Society, and Culture*. Reno: Center for Basque Studies, 2003.

Andoni, Alonso, and Iñaki Arzoz. *Basque Cyberculture: From Digital Euskadi to CyberEuskalherria*. Reno: Center for Basque Studies, 2003.

Aresti, Gabriel. *Downhill and Rock & Core*. Translated by Amaia Gabantxo. Reno: Center for Basque Studies, 2016.

Arrizabalaga, Marie-Pierre. "A Statistical Study of Basque Immigration into California, Nevada, Idaho, and Wyoming between 1900–1910." Master's thesis, University of Nevada, Reno, September, 1986.

Astrain, Luis Nunez. *The Basques: Their Struggle for Independence*. Wales: Welsh Academic Press, 1997.

Ault, Jody. "Unraveling of Identity: The Search for Basques in French and Spanish Histories." Master of Applied Historical Research project, Boise State University, 2008.

Berriochoa, Kattalina Marie. "Saving Euskara." In *Becoming Basque: Ethnic Heritage on Boise's Grove Street*. Edited by John Bieter, Dave Lachiondo, and John Ysursa, 31–47. Boise: Boise State University, Investigate Boise Community Research Series, 2014.

Berry, Kate and Martha L. Henderson, eds. *Geographical Identities of Ethnic America*. Reno: University of Nevada Press, 2002.

Bieter, J. Patrick. "Pete Cenarrusa: Idaho's Champion of Basque Culture." In *Portraits of Basques in the New World*, edited by Richard Etulain and Jeronomia Echeverria. Reno: University of Nevada Press, 1999.

Bieter, J. Patrick. "Reluctant Shepherds: The Basques in Idaho." In *Idaho Yesterdays* 1 (1957): 10–15.

———. "Letemendi's Boarding House: A Basque Cultural Institution in Idaho." In *Idaho Yesterdays* 37: 1 (Spring 1993).

———. "Basques in Idaho." In Idaho Yesterdays 41 (Summer 1997): 22–32.

Bieter, John P. "Basques, Basque-Americans, American-Basques: Three Generations of Basques in Boise." Master's thesis, Boise State University, 1994.

Bieter, John, and Mark Bieter. *An Enduring Legacy: The Story of Basques in Idaho*. Reno: University of Nevada Press, 2000.

Bieter, John, and Mark Bieter. "Boise's Wrigley Field." In *Becoming Basque: Ethnic Heritage on Boise's Grove Street*. Edited by John Bieter, Dave Lachiondo, and John Ysursa, 65–83. Boise: Boise State University, Investigate Boise Community Research Series, 2014.

BIBLIOGRAPHY

Bieter, John, Dave Lachiondo, and John Ysursa, eds. *Becoming Basque: Ethnic Heritage on Boise's Grove Street*. Boise: Boise State University, Investigate Boise Community Research Series, 2014.

Bilbao, Julio. "Basque Names in Early Idaho." In *Basques of the Pacific Northwest*. Edited by Richard Etulain. Pocatello: Idaho State University Press, 1991.

Blain, Angeline Kearns. "Juanita 'Jay' Uberuaga Hormaechea and the Boise Heritage School of Basque Dancing." In *Portraits of Basques in the New World*. Reno: University of Nevada Press, 1999.

Boise State University, Basque Studies Program. "Basque Scholar Feature: Jon Bilbao." In *BOGA: Basque Studies Consortium Journal* 2, issue 1 (October 2014).

Boyd, Robert G., William A. Douglass, Richard W. Etulain, Jeronima Echeverria, Robert Echeverria, Thomas McClanahan, David Romtvedt, and Linda White. *Amerikanuak! Basques in the High Desert*. Bend: High Desert Museum and the Idaho Humanities Foundation, 1995.

Bradley, Cyprian, Rt. Rev., and Edward J. Kelly, Most. Rev. *History of the Diocese of Boise, 1863–1952*, Volume 1. Boise: Roman Catholic Diocese of Boise, 1953.

Brusen, Bernice. *Basques from the Pyrenees to the Rockies*. Portland: Dynagraphics Printing, 1985.

Clark, Robert P. *The Basques: The Franco Years and Beyond*. Reno: University of Nevada Press, 1979.

Coon, Heidi. "Jay's Jota." In *Becoming Basque: Ethnic Heritage on Boise's Grove Street*. Edited by John Bieter, Dave Lachiondo, and John Ysursa, 117–127. Boise: Boise State University, Investigate Boise Community Research Series, 2014.

Demo, Pam. "Boise's River Street Neighborhood: Lee, Ash, and Lovers Lane/Pioneer Streets: The South Side of the Tracks." Master's thesis, University of Idaho, April, 2006.

Diner, Hasia R. *Erin's Daughters in America: Irish Immigrant Women in the Nineteenth Century*. Baltimore: Johns Hopkins University Press, 1983.

———. *Hungering for America: Italian, Irish, and Jewish Foodways in the Age of Immigration*. Cambridge: Harvard University Press, 2001.

Dougherty, Argia Beristain. "Women in Basque Nationalism." Course lectures at Boise State University, Fall 2014.

Douglass, William A. "Foreword." In *Sweet Promised Land*, Robert Laxalt. Reno: University of Nevada Press, 1986 — reprint of the 1957 edition, New York: Harper & Row.

———. Basque Festival." In *Basques of the Pacific Northwest*. Edited by Richard Etulain. Pocatello: Idaho State University Press, 1991.

———. "Basques in the American West." In *To Build in a New Land: Ethnic Landscapes in North America*. Edited by Allen G. Noble. Baltimore and London: The Johns Hopkins University Press, 1992.

———. *Global Vasconia: Essays on the Basque Diaspora*. Reno: Center for Basque Studies, 2007.

———. "Basque Immigration in the United States." *BOGA Basque Studies Consortium Journal* 1, issue 1, article 5 (October 2013).

Douglass, William A. and Jon Bilbao. *Amerikanuak: Basques in the New World*. Reno: University of Nevada Press, 1975.

BIBLIOGRAPHY

Douglass, William A., Richard W. Etulain, and William H. Jacobsen, Jr., eds. "Anglo-American Contributions to Basque Studies: Essays in honor of Jon Bilbao." *Desert Research Institute Publications on the Social Sciences,* No. 13, 1977.

Douglass, William A. and Richard H. Lane. B*asque Sheepherders of the American West.* Reno: University of Nevada Press, 1985.

Douglass, William A. and Joseba Zulaika. "Auzolan." In B*asque Culture: Anthropological Perspectives.* Reno: University of Nevada, Center for Basque Studies, 2007.

Dubos, René, "The Spirit of Place." In *A God Within.* New York: Charles Scribner's Sons, 1972.

Echeverria, Begoña. "For Whom Does Language Death Toll? Cautionary Tales from the Basque Case." *Linguistics and Education* 21 (2010): 197–209.

Echeverria, Jeronima. *Home Away from Home: A History of Basque Boarding Houses.* Reno: University of Nevada Press, 1999.

———. *Home Off the Range: Basque Hotels of the American West.* Salt Lake City: University of Utah, Graduate School of Architecture, 1999.

———. "Lyda Esain: A Hotelera's Story." In *Portraits of Basques in the New World.* Edited by Richard W. Etulain and Jeronima Echeverria. Reno: University of Nevada Press, 1999.

———. "Home Away from Home." In E*txea: The Cyrus Jacobs-Uberuaga House.* Edited by Meggan Laxalt Mackey. Boise: Basque Museum and Cultural Center, 2010.

Edelfsen, John B. "A Sociological Study of the Basques of Southwest Idaho." Ph.D. dissertation, State College of Washington, 1938.

Eidson, Kyle, and Dave Lachiondo. "Reclaiming the Flag." In *Becoming Basque: Ethnic Heritage on Boise's Grove Street.* Edited by John Bieter, Dave Lachiondo, and John Ysursa, 169–185. Boise: Boise State University, Investigate Boise Community Research Series, 2014.

Etulain, Richard W., and Jeronima Echeverria, eds. *Portaits of Basques in the New World.* Reno: University of Nevada Press, 1999.

Etulain, Richard, ed. *Basques of the Pacific Northwest.* Pocatello: Idaho State University Press, 1991.

———. "Introduction," and "Basque Beginnings in the Pacific Northwest." In *Basques of the Pacific Northwest.* Pocatello: Idaho State University Press, 1991.

Etxegoien, Juan Carlos "Xamar." *Orhipean: The Country of Basque.* Pamplona-Iruna: Udalbide, 2001.

Forni, Gianfranco. "Evidence for Basque as an Indo-European Language." *Journal of Indo-European Studies* 41, no. 1 and 3 (Spring/Summer 2013).

Galdos, Imanol Irazabal, "Boise: The Future of the Basque Country." Paper presentation at *Joan Etorri: Going Back and Forth,* Basque Studies Symposium hosted by Boise State University Basque Studies Program and the Etxepare Basque Institute, Jaialdi 2015, July 29, 2015.

Gallop, Rodney. *A Book of the Basques.* London: MacMillan Publishing, 1930; Reprinted Reno: University of Nevada Press, 1970.

BIBLIOGRAPHY

Gans, Herbert J. "Symbolic Ethnicity: The Future of Ethnic Groups and Cultures in America." *Ethnic and Racial Studies* 2, no. 1, January (1979): 1–20.

———. "Symbolic Ethnicity and Symbolic Religiosity: Towards a Comparison of Ethnic and Religious Acculturation." *Ethnic and Racial Studies* 17, no. 4 (October 1994): 577–92.

———. "The Coming Darkness of Late-Generation European American Ethnicity." *Ethnic and Racial Studies* 37, no. 5 (June 2014): 757–65.

Glotfelty, Cheryll. *Literary Nevada: Writings from the Silver State*. Reno: University of Nevada Press, 2008.

Gorrell, Nikki. "An Educational Program for the Basque Museum: A Series of Recommendations." Master's thesis, Boise State University, May 2008.

Green, Michael, ed. "Basque Environmental History Issue." *Nevada Historical Quarterly* 52, no. 4, Winter (2009). Special edition includes articles by John Bieter, "Forrest Gump was Basque: Prospects for Basque Environmental History;" Amahia Mallea, "Enduring Conflicts and Cooperation;" D. Seth Murray, "The Contested Spaces of the Basque Countryside;" Michael Baldrica and Carrie Smith "Research, Management, and Interpretation of Historic Sheep Camps on the East Side of the Tahoe National Forest;" Joe Odiaga, "We Were Not Tramp Sheepmen" and Kevin D. Hatfield "Acculturation, Resistance and Identity in the Bizkaian Basque Community, 1890–1946."

Groth, Paul and Todd W. Bressi, eds. *Understanding Ordinary Landscapes*. New Haven: Yale University Press, 1997.

Halter, Marilyn. *Shopping for Identity: The Marketing of Ethnicity*. New York: Schocken Books, 2000.

Handlin, Oscar. *The Uprooted*. Boston: Atlantic Monthly Press — Little, Brown and Company, 1951, 1973.

———. *The Children of the Uprooted*. New York: Braziller, 1966.

Hansen, Marcus Lee. "The Problem of the Third Generation Immigrant." In *The Children of the Uprooted*. Edited by Oscar Handlin. New York: Braziller, 1966.

Hardesty, Liz (Arregui-Dick). "The Unmarked Basque Graves Project." *IGS Quarterly* (Autumn 1998).

Hardwick, Susan. "Russians in the Sacramento Valley." In *Homelands: A Geography of Culture and Place Across America*. Edited by Richard L. Nostrand and Lawrence E. Estaville. Baltimore: Johns Hopkins University Press, 2001.

Hayden, Dolores. *The Power of Place: Urban Landscapes as Public History*. Cambridge, MA: The MIT Press, 1995.

Hill-Marino, Gretchen. "Production of Heritage: The Basque Block in Boise, Idaho." *BOGA Basque Studies Consortium Journal* 1, issue 2 (2014): 1–22.

———. "Inventing the Basque Block: Heritage Tourism and Identity Politics in Boise, Idaho." Master's thesis, University of Oregon Graduate School, Department of Geography, September 2012.

Hualde, José Ignacio and Koldo Zuazo. "The Standardization of the Basque Language." *Language Problems and Language Planning* 31.2 (2007).

Hualde, José Ignacio, Joseba A. Lakarra, and R.L. Trask, eds. *Towards a History of the Basque Language*. Amsterdam: John Benjamins Publishing, 1995.

Hummer, Christine. "Basque Center." In *Becoming Basque: Ethnic Heritage on Boise's Grove Street*. Edited by John Bieter, Dave Lachiondo, and John Ysursa, 157–67. Boise: Boise State University, Investigate Boise Community Research Series, 2014.

BIBLIOGRAPHY

Irujo Ametzaga, Xabier. *Expelled From the Motherland*. Reno: Center for Basque Studies, 2012.

———. *On Basque Politics: Conversations with Pete Cenarrusa*. Brussels: European Research Institute, 2009.

Jackson, John Brinckerhoff (J. B.). *Discovering the Vernacular Landscape*. New Haven: Yale University Press, 1984.

———. *The Necessity for Ruins and Other Topics*. Amherst: University of Massachusetts Press, 1990.

———. *A Sense of Place, A Sense of Time*. New Haven: Yale University Press, 1994.

———. *Landscape in Sight: Looking at America*. Edited by Helen Lefkowitz Horowitz. New Haven: Yale University Press, 1997.

———. "The Moveable Dwelling and How It Came to America." In *Landscape in Sight*. Edited by Helen Lefkowitz Horowitz. New Haven: Yale University Press, 1997.

James, Ronald M. "Community on the Comstock: Cliché, Stereotype, and Reality in the Mining West." In *Community in the American West*. Edited by Stephen Tchudi. Reno: Nevada Humanities Committee, 1999.

Kasinitz, Phillip. "Herbert Gans and the Death of Miss Norway." *Ethnic and Racial Studies* 37, no. 5 (2014): 770–73.

Kennedy, John F. *A Nation of Immigrants*. New York: Harper & Row, 1964.

Kurlansky, Mark. *The Basque History of the World: The Story of a Nation*. New York: Walker Books, 1999. Later reprint by Penguin Books, 2001.

Kyvig, David E., Myron A. Marty, and the American Association of State and Local History. *Nearby History: Exploring the Past around You*. Lanham, Maryland: AltaMira Press, 2010.

Laxalt, Robert. *Sweet Promised Land*. New York: Harper & Row, 1957.

———. *In a Hundred Graves*. Reno: University of Nevada Press, 1972.

———. *The Basque Hotel*. Reno: University of Nevada Press, 1989.

———. *Child of the Holy Ghost*. Reno: University of Nevada Press, 1992.

———. *Land of My Fathers: A Son's Return to the Basque Country*. Reno: University of Nevada Press, 1999.

Laxalt Mackey, Meggan, ed. *Etxea: The Cyrus Jacobs-Uberuaga House*. Boise: Basque Museum and Cultural Center, 2010.

———. "Cultural Landmarks." In *Becoming Basque: Ethnic Heritage on Boise's Grove Street*. Edited by John Bieter, Dave Lachiondo, and John Ysursa, 99–115. Boise: Boise State University, Investigate Boise Community Research Series, 2014.

Laxalt [Jensen] Mackey, Meggan and Michelle Hall, Suzanne Sermon. *Eden to Asphalt: A Landscape Analysis Boise's Grove Street*. Boise: Boise State University, 1994.

Laxalt Urza, Monique. *Deep Blue Memory*. Reno: University of Nevada Press, 1993.

Lerude, Warren. *Robert Laxalt: The Story of a Storyteller*. Reno: University of Nevada Press, 2013.

Lewis, Peirce. "The Monument and the Bungalow: The Intellectual Legacy of J.B. Jackson." In *Everyday America: Cultural Landscape Studies after J.B. Jackson*. Edited by Chris Wilson and Paul Groth. Berkeley: University of California Press, 2003.

Limerick, Patricia Nelson. *The Legacy of Conquest: The Unbroken Past of the American West*. New York: WW Norton and Company, 1987.

BIBLIOGRAPHY

Malea-Olaetxe, José. *Speaking through the Aspens: Basque Tree Carvings in Nevada and California*. Reno: University of Nevada Press, 2008.

Meinig, D. W., J. B. Jackson, Peirce F. Lewis, David Lowenthal, Marwyn Samuels, David E. Sopher, and Yi-Fu Tuan. *The Interpretation of Ordinary Landscapes*. New York: Oxford University Press, 1979.

Miller, Patty A. "They Made This Their Home." In *Etxea: The Cyrus Jacobs-Uberuaga House*. Edited by Meggan Laxalt Mackey. Boise: Basque Museum and Cultural Center, 2010.

Mitxelena, Koldo. *Koldo Mitxelena: Selected Writings of a Basque Scholar*. Reno: University of Nevada, Center for Basque Studies, Basque Classics Series, no. 4, 2008.

Noble, Allen G., ed. *To Build in a New Land: Ethnic Landscapes in North America*. Baltimore and London: The Johns Hopkins University Press, 1992.

Nostrand, Richard L. and Lawrence E. Estaville, eds. *Homelands: A Geography of Culture and Place Across America*. Baltimore: Johns Hopkins University Press, 2001.

Oiarzabal, Pedro J. *A Candle in the Night: Basque Studies at the University of Nevada*. Reno: University of Nevada, Oral History Program, 2007.

———. *Gardeners of Identity: Basques in the San Francisco Bay Area*. Reno: Center for Basque Studies, 2009.
    Oldenburg, Ray. *The Great Good Place: Cafés, Coffee shops, Bookstores, Bars, Hair Salons, and Other Hangouts at the Heart of a Community*. New York: Marlowe and Company, 1999.

———. *Celebrating the Third Place: Inspiring Stories about the "Great Good Places" at the Heart of Our Communities*. Boston: De Capo Press, 2001.

Ott, Sandra. T*he Circle of Mountains: Basque Sheepherding and Community*. Reno: University of Nevada Press, 1981.

Pacyga, Dominic A. *Polish Immigrants and Industrial Chicago: Workers on the South Side, 1880–1922*. Chicago: University of Chicago Press, 1991, 2003.

Paseman, Susan. "Church of the Good Shepherd." In *Becoming Basque: Ethnic Heritage on Boise's Grove Street*. Edited by John Bieter, Dave Lachiondo, and John Ysursa, 49–63. Boise: Boise State University, Investigate Boise Community Research Series, 2014.

Phinney, Jean S. "A Three-Stage Model of Ethnic Identity Development in Adolescence." In *Ethnic Identity: Formation and Transmission among Hispanics and Other Minorities*. Edited by Martha E. Bernal and George P. Knight. Albany: State University of New York Press, 1993.

Rio, David. *Robert Laxalt: The Voice of the Basques of American Literature*. Reno: Center for Basque Studies, 2007.

———. "Monique Laxalt: A Literary Interpreter for the New Generations of Basque-Americans." In *Amatxi, Amuma, Amona: Writings in Honor of Basque Women*. Edited by Linda White and Cameron Watson. Reno: University of Nevada, Center for Basque Studies, 2003.

Romtvedt, David and Dollie Iberlin, eds. *Buffalotarrak: An Anthology of the Basques of Buffalo, Wyoming*. 2nd edition. Reno: Center for Basque Studies, , 2011.

Sather, Clifford A. "Marriage Patterns Among the Basques of Shoshone, Idaho," Master's thesis, Reed College, 1961. In "Basques, Basque-Americans, American Basques," *John Bieter Master's thesis*, April 1994.

Schnell, Steven M. "Creating Narratives of Place and Identity in Little Sweden, USA." *The Geographical Review* 93, no. 1 (January 2003): 1–29.

BIBLIOGRAPHY

Shallat, Todd. *Ethnic Landmarks: Ten Places that Define the City of Trees*. Boise: City of Boise and Boise State University College of Social Sciences and Public Affairs, 2007.

Shelby, Jennifer. "Remaking Grove." In *Becoming Basque: Ethnic Heritage on Boise's Grove Street*. Edited by John Bieter, Dave Lachiondo, and John Ysursa, 187–203. Boise: Boise State University, Investigate Boise Community Research Series, 2014.

Stilgoe, John. *Borderland: Origins of the American Suburb, 1820–1939; The Common Landscape of America, 1580–1845; Outside Lies Magic: Discovering History and Inspiration in Ordinary Places*. New York: WW Norton and Company, 1987; New Haven: Yale University Press, 1982.

Strauss, Paul, Patricia Nelson Limerick, Helen Lefkowitz Horowitz, Peirce Lewis, and Gwendolyn Wright, eds. "Special Edition Dedicated to J. B. Jackson." *Geographical Review* 88, no. 4 (October 1998).

Sullivan, Thomas. "'I Want to Be All I Can Irish': The Role of Performance and Performativity in the Construction of Ethnicity." *Social and Cultural Geography* 13, no. 5 (August 2012): 429–44.

Tchudi, Stephen, ed. *Community in the American West*. Reno and Las Vegas: Nevada Humanities Committee, 1999.

Totoricaguena, Gloria Pilar. *Boise Basques: Dreamers and Doers*. Reno: Center for Basque Studies, 2004.

———. *Identity, Culture and Politics in the Basque Diaspora*. Reno: Center for Basque Studies, 2004.

———. *Basque Diaspora: Migration and Transnational Identity*. Reno: Center for Basque Studies, 2005.

———. *The Basques of New York: A Cosmopolitan Experience*. Reno: Center for Basque Studies, 2004.

Trask, R. L. *History of the Basque*. New York/London: Routledge, 1996.

Tyler, Norman, Ted. J. Ligibel, and Ilene R. Taylor. *Historical Preservation: An Introduction to Its History, Principles, and Practices*. New York: W.W. Norton & Company, 2009.

Urza, Carmelo. *Solitude: Art and Symbolism in the National Basque Monument*. Reno: University of Nevada Press, 1993.

———. "The Age of Institutions: Basques in the U.S." In *Community in the American West*. Edited by Stephen Tchudi, Reno and Las Vegas: Nevada Humanities Committee, vol. 21, (1999): 231-251.

Villanueva, José. *Archived collection of letters, papers, publications, music sheets and other personal effects*. Basque Museum and Cultural Center. Boise Idaho: Basque Museum and Cultural Center; accessed October, 2014.

Waters, Mary. *Ethnic Options: Choosing Identities in America*. Berkeley: University of California Press, 1990.

———. "Ethnic identities in the future: the possible effects of mass immigration and genetic testing." *Ethnic and Racial Studies* 37, no. 5, (2014): 766–69.

White, Linda and Cameron Watson, eds. *Amatxi, Amuma, Amona: Writings in Honor of Basque Women*. Reno: Center for Basque Studies, 2003.

Wilson, Chris and Paul Groth, eds. *Everyday America: Cultural Landscape Studies After J. B. Jackson*. Berkeley: University of California Press, 2003.

Woodworth, Paddy. *The Basque Country: A Cultural History*. Landscapes of the Imagination Series. Oxford: Oxford University Press, 2008.

———. "Foreword." In *Gardeners of Identity: Basques in the San Francisco Bay Area*, ed. Pedro Oiarzabal. Reno: Center for Basque Studies, 2009.

BIBLIOGRAPHY

Ysursa, John P. "Invisible Cargo." In E*txea: The Cyrus Jacobs-Uberuaga House*. Edited by Meggan Laxalt Mackey. Boise: Basque Museum and Cultural Center, 2010.

Zube, Ervin H. *Landscapes: Selected Writings of J. B. Jackson*. Boston: University of Massachusetts Press, 1970.

Zubiri, Nancy. *Travel Guide to Basque America: Families, Feasts and Festivals*. Reno: University of Nevada Press, 2006.

TIMELINE PHOTO CREDITS

Basque cave paintings: Ekaiberri Cave horses	www.alamy.com
Biscay Basque whaling print	Gipuzcoa Geroztik Historia museo birtuala
Fueros	Digital online search
Linguae Vasconum Primitae title page	University of Nevada, Reno
Declaration of Independence painting	www.britannica.com by John Trumbull
Bill of Rights	Digital online search
French Revolution painting, Liberty	www.rjgeib.com/thoughts/ leading the People, by Eugene Delacroix
First Carlist War photograph	www.moddb.com www.theeapricity.com
Les Carlistes, print	www.wikiwand.com
California Gold Rush	en.wikipedia.org
Boise 1863	www.boiseartsandhistoryorg
Fort Boise	Fort Boise Historical Association
Transcontinental Railroad	en.wikipedia.org
Chinese? No! No! No! poster 1892	www.mocanyc.org
Idaho silver miners photograph	Inland Northwest
Idaho state seal 1890	www.sos.idaho.gov
Gestal/Spanish Restaurant, Boise	Basque Museum and Cultural Center Arthur Hart article, *Idaho Statesman*
Sabino Arana	blogs.deia.com
Ikurriña	Clipart
Spanish-American War 1898 poster	www.travelphotobase.com

TIMELINE PHOTO CREDITS

Ellis Island building	en.wikipedia.com
Ellis Island immigrants	teacher.scholastic.com
Basque sheepcamp	University of Nevada, Reno
Fr. Bernardo Arregui	Basque Museum and Cultural Center
Centro Vasco Americano, 1913, New York	espanyu.org
Anduiza Fronton	"Boise by Burns," Basque Museum and Cultural Center
World War I soldiers	myinterestingfacts.com
Church of the Good Shepherd	Basque Museum and Cultural Center
Juan Anduiza	Basque Museum and Cultural Center
Emergency Quota Act anti-Japanese photo	amhistory.si.edu
Taylor Grazing act - on the range	Laxalt Family
Depression era	Digital online search
Sheepherder's Ball	Basque Museum and Cultural Center
Picasso's "Guernica" (Gernika) Mural	ksarts.com
World War II bomber plane photograph	en.wikipedia.com
"Song of the Basques" program 1949	Basque Museum and Cultural Center
Basque Center c.1950	Basque Museum and Cultural Center
Korean War LIFE magazine cover	donmoorewartales.com
Vietnam War demonstrators photo	en.wikipedia.com
Sweet Promised Land book jacket 1957	Meggan Laxalt Mackey
First Basque Festival, Sparks, Nevada 1959	University of Nevada, Reno

TIMELINE PHOTO CREDITS

Boise Oinkari Dancers at World's Fair 1964	Basque Museum and Cultural Center
President John F. Kennedy photograph 1963	en.wikipedia.com
Rev. Martin Luther King photograph 1968	CBSlocal.com
Boise Basque Holiday Festival program 1972	Basque Museum and Cultural Center
NABO logo	North American Basque Organizations
Boise-Oñati Study Abroad Program	Boise State University, Basque Studies
Amerikanuak book title page 1975	Meggan Laxalt Mackey
Roots book jacket 1977	www.prweb.com
Jacobs Boardinghouse, 607 Grove St.	Basque Museum and Cultural Center
Jaialdi 1987 program	Meggan Laxalt Mackey
Basque Museum & Cultural Center	Basque Museum and Cultural Center
Cub Bar sign	Basque Museum and Cultural Center
Bar Gernika	Meggan Laxalt Mackey
Anduiza Fronton interior	"Boise by Burns," Basque Museum and Cultural Center
Jaialdi 1995 program	Meggan Laxalt Mackey
Boiseko Ikastola logo	Basque Museum and Cultural Center
An Enduring Legacy, John and Mark Bieter	Meggan Laxalt Mackey
Portraits of Basques, Etulain and Echeverria	Meggan Laxalt Mackey
Basque Block laiak sculpture	Meggan Laxalt Mackey
Jaialdi 2005 program	Meggan Laxalt Mackey
Boise State University Basque Studies logo	Boise State University, Basque Studies
Jaialdi 2010, Oinkari Basque Dancers	www.Oinkari.org

TIMELINE PHOTO CREDITS

ETA motto	en.wikipedia.com
Anduiza Fronton 100th Anniversary card	Meggan Laxalt Mackey
Artzai Ona Basque Catholic Community logo	Peter Laxalt
Boise Basque Soccer Friendly Logo 2015	Basque Soccer Friendly
Joan Etorri Symposium program Boise State University, Jaialdi 2015	Boise State University Basque Studies Meggan Laxalt Mackey
Jaialdi 2015 program	Meggan Laxalt Mackey
Ahaztu Barik logo	Meggan Laxalt Mackey
Etxepare Basque Institute logo	Etxepare Basque Institute
University of the Basque Country logo	University of the Basque Country
Basque Museum Exhibits, Promo Materials	Basque Museum and Cultural Center
Boiseko Ikastola	Basque Museum and Cultural Center

www.ingramcontent.com/pod-product-compliance
Lightning Source LLC
Chambersburg PA
CBHW060925170426

43192CB00024B/2893